T0329257

# WAGES AND INCOME
# IN THE UNITED KINGDOM

# WAGES AND INCOME

## IN THE UNITED KINGDOM
## SINCE 1860

by

A. L. BOWLEY, C.B.E., Sc.D., F.B.A.

*Emeritus Professor of Statistics in the*
*University of London*

CAMBRIDGE
AT THE UNIVERSITY PRESS
1937

# Contents

NOTE. The numbered references in the text, thus (ref. 74), refer to the numbered Bibliography, pp. 142 *seq.*

# Introduction

This book is an attempt to bring into a coherent whole the investigations that I have made on the subjects of wages and income at various dates during the past forty years. Some of the more essential studies are out of print and others are not very easily accessible. Also as information has accumulated and additional analyses have been made, earlier estimates have been modified, and different classifications have been used for special purposes, so that some confusion might arise for anyone who wished to find my estimates over any long period. The plan often adopted of re-issuing in collected form a group of papers and essays did not appear to be suitable, or indeed practicable in view of the expense. The elaborate statistical tables, on which the results are based, are better left to the serious student who may be working at a special aspect of wage or price movements, and for his use a bibliography is included, by the help of which he can work back to the data and follow the technical processes of analysis; for, as in all fields of statistics, there is a special technique for analysing wages and another for measuring prices. When the originals are in Journals that are to be found in the usual Libraries, it has only been necessary to indicate the methods and to quote the results; but when the originals are out of print or in less obvious publications, more detail has been included in the text. It has not always been easy to re-examine and justify statistics which were handled thirty or more years ago, or to recover the exact classifications employed. Full detail can rarely be given in any reasonable space for statistics of this kind, and something depends on judgment and general knowledge of the material that cannot be completely justified in argument. Occasionally in using the earlier papers the clue has not been recoverable, and I have thought it better not to try to amend the estimate but to give it with the tacit assumption that comparability had been preserved in the series given.

For the essence of these studies is not the obtaining of absolute totals, but the measurement of changes. Absolute totals depend on the definitions of such classes as income (individual and national), wages, earnings, unemployment, occupation, working and middle class, cost of living, standard of living, poverty. In each case there is an element of arbitrariness in definition or classification. In stating the numbers in the 'middle class', definition is reached by delimitation, as in the code-numbers of the Census, listed on p. 133. For national income it is necessary to state separately many items, and to choose which are appropriate for combination to correspond with this or that definition. But much of this difficulty is evaded in comparison. So long as precisely the same definition and the same classification are preserved, it is usually indifferent on which side of a line relatively small marginal quantities are placed; the rate of change is hardly affected. More important is the consideration that while very varying estimates may be made by different investigators for one date, the change shown over a period is definite if the method and classifications are the same throughout it. Very important illustrations of this principle are to be found in wage and also in price statistics.

In the end our results can be only approximate, however exact our definitions. Very often there is no information about some integral part of a total. For example, in estimating aggregate wages or earnings we know almost nothing about the payments to shop assistants or to resident or non-resident domestic servants. In total income there is a gap between those who are assessed to income-tax and wage-earners which can only be filled over long periods by hazardous interpolation. The fitting in the sporadic information that exists on such subjects is a matter of judgment rather than one of arithmetic. We can only proceed, if we can ascertain the maximum disturbance that variance of such estimates can have on our results. It is ridiculous to give any of the major totals to several digits, as if they were known to one part even in a thousand.[1] Estimates should always carry with them an indication of the margin of uncertainty to which they are subject. Sometimes such a margin can be fixed because there are estimates on alternative bases and by different investigators, as the National Income can be built up either from production or from income statistics, with resultant differences of perhaps 10 per cent. The situation is rather different when the results are in the form of index-numbers. They may be expected to be accurate, within their definitions, within 1 or 2 per cent. over short periods, say of five years, if the changes have not been too sudden or abnormal; over longer periods the errors may be cumulative, and it may be proper to allow a 10 per cent. margin. But they serve an important end if they allow us only to show the dates of change, to state that the thing measured was greater or less at one period than at another, and to distinguish violent fluctuations from slight oscillations.

In a summary book of this kind it has not been possible, or even desirable, to exhibit much detail or analysis of the accuracy of the sources, which are to be found in the originals. Where necessary an indication is given of the margin to be assigned to the estimates. The more technical matter and the collation with former estimates are relegated to the notes in the Appendices.

In revising former work the opportunity has been taken of bringing some of the series up-to-date, so that the wages include the results of the 1935 enquiry, and wage and price index-numbers continue to the end of 1936. I have not attempted, however, an estimate of National Income since 1924, but only given some of the more important constituents in subsequent years.

At one time I thought of giving this work the more ambitious title 'The Condition of the People', which was the nominal subject of the Marshall lectures given at Cambridge in the autumn of 1935 and incorporated to a considerable extent in the

[1] In preliminary working and even in the final tables it is often convenient to keep more digits than are ultimately justified.

subsequent chapters. Another possible title was 'Progress of the Working Class'. On reflection neither seemed to be suitable. The word Progress prejudges the results; it might be that there was retrogression. Also the idea of progress is largely psychological and certainly relative; people are apt to measure their progress not from a forgotten position in the past, but towards an ideal, which, like an horizon, continually recedes. The present generation is not interested in the earlier needs and successes of its progenitors, but in its own distresses and frustration considered in the light of the presumed possibility of universal comfort or riches. The standard of living may rise considerably, but only over a long period; its change is not perceptible to a growing generation, which knows that its own means are insufficient for its desires.[1] The Condition of the People implies that 'the people' are a class within the nation, while one of the main changes, shown by the statistics and otherwise evident, is that lines of division are being obliterated, and there is a continual graduation from the poorest to the richest both in wealth and habits. More important is that on the statistical side there are many measurements of health, attention to social services, education, crime and other subjects, such as are considered for example in *The New Survey of London Life and Labour*, which I have not specially studied and have not dealt with in the sequel; and also many incommensurables, such as advantage of leisure, the increasing urbanisation of the population, the varying intensity or disagreeableness of work, the increasing variety of entertainment and facilities for travel, all of which are germane to the description of the well-being of the population. On the plea that the pedestrian statistician should stick to his last, this work is confined to the measurable framework within which the pursuit of happiness takes place.

In 1886 Giffen read to the Statistical Society a paper entitled

[1] 'My plight is, alas, worse for—I cannot lay hands on more than £500 (per annum), and that in this country spells mere existence, if that.' Quoted in the *New Statesman* from a letter to *The Times*, in the autumn of 1935.

'Further Notes on the Progress of the Working Classes'; he says: 'I doubt whether much could be added to the triple and quadruple chain of evidence by which the great progress of the working classes in the last half century is proved. The great rise of money wages among labourers of every class, coupled with stationary or even falling prices of commodities on the average, the all but universal shortening of hours of labour, the decline of pauperism, the enormously increased consumption of the luxuries of the masses, the improvement in the rate of mortality—these and other facts combine to prove that there has been a great general advance in well-being among the masses of the community.'

And again: 'The general conclusion from the facts is, that what has happened to the working classes in the last fifty years is not so much what may properly be called an improvement, as a revolution of the most remarkable description. The new possibilities implied in changes which in fifty years have sub-stituted for millions of people in the United Kingdom who were constantly on the brink of starvation, and who suffered untold privations, new millions of artisans and fairly well-paid labourers, ought indeed to excite the hopes of philanthropists and public men. From being a dependent class without future or hope, the masses of working men have got into a position from which they may effectually advance to almost any degree of civilisation. . . . The working men have the game in their own hands. Education and thrift, which they can achieve for them-selves, will, if necessary, do all that remains to be done.' Quoted from *Essays in Finance*, Second Series, pp. 409 and 473 (ref. 75).

No doubt the condition of 'the masses' in 1836 was deplor-able in the extreme. But was the level implied by these words in 1886 one that we should now contemplate with equanimity? Three years after this paper was read Booth began his *Survey of London Life and Labour*, and found that one-third of the working class was below his poverty line—a line which is now regarded as a very undesirable minimum.

Would a repetition of Giffen's words give a true account for the further half-century that has elapsed since he spoke them?

In a large measure the answer is yes. Wages have increased more than have prices. The rise in the fifty years has been greatest in the classes where improvement was most needed. Hours of labour have greatly diminished; the so-called masses consume more of what Giffen termed luxuries (sugar, tea, tobacco), and have a greatly increased variety of amusements, many of them of recent invention, on which the increased margin of income over necessaries can be spent. The rate of mortality has progressively fallen till there seems to be little room for it to fall further. Pauperism in his sense is no longer an adequate measurement of poverty. His paupers, which amounted in 1881 to 31 per thousand of the population, have been replaced by 'persons in receipt of Institutional or Domiciliary relief'. These were 33 per thousand of the population of England and Wales in 1935, but the very great majority of these, 29, had 'domiciliary' relief, due to unemployment, a subject with which Giffen did not deal. There are new millions of well or 'fairly well-paid' artisans and labourers, that is, well paid on the standard current fifty years ago. Their representatives state in their election programmes that if 'the game' is put into 'their hands' the people can 'effectually advance to a much higher degree of prosperity'. But though many of the working class are well educated (in comparison shall we say with the middle class) thrift is not a conspicuous part of their programme.

The subsequent chapters show statistical details of some of the changes in the past fifty years. Before summarising them it may be well to look back to a rather earlier period, for which statistics are incomplete but sufficient to show the tendencies. Mr G. H. Wood's estimate of average wages from 1850 (ref. 86) shows a rapid rise in money wages from 1853 to 1855, induced by the high prices of the Crimean War, and more than neutralised by their rise. After some relapse a further rise in money wages began after 1858 and continued with little interruption till its culmination in 1874. Prices were also rising, at some dates sharply, in this period, so that there was a set-back in real wages from 1865 to 1868. From 1874 to 1879 prices fell fast, and wages at nearly the same rate. Wood's figures for *real* wages (ignoring changes in unemployment), the basis of which is explained below (p. 123), give for the approximate dates of maxima and minima and some other years:

| | | | |
|---|---|---|---|
| 1850 | 100 | 1867 | 109 |
| 1855 | 95 | 1876 | 137 |
| 1861 | 100 | 1880 | 134 |
| 1864–5 | 117 | 1886 | 151 |

Thus Giffen's contention of considerable progress is supported for at least the latter half of his period.

The basic point for this book is chosen as 1880, by which date the figures are sufficient for fairly precise statements. It also falls within a short period during which the changes of wages and prices were small. Then three periods are studied: 1880 to 1914, 1914 to 1924, and 1924 to 1937. The essential estimates of the movement of wages and prices are given in index-number form in the table on p. 30.

As regards the first period, it will be seen there that money earnings rose throughout the thirty-five years, with slight relapses in 1884, 1900–2 and 1908, together with periods of stationariness. Over the whole the average increase was nearly 1 per cent. per annum. The 'cost of living' fell with some interruptions from 1880 (and indeed from 1873) to a minimum in 1895–6, and then rose with one set-back till 1907, reaching approximately the level that was recovered, after a slight fall, in 1914. When we make the familiar, but rough, estimate of the movement of real wages by applying the cost of living index to the wage-index, we obtain a sequence of quite a different character. Real wages are seen to rise rapidly from 1880 to a temporary maximum in 1895–6, increasing by some 40 per cent. in fifteen years, and then to oscillate about that maximum for nearly twenty years. Since it is doubtful exactly at what dates in the 'nineties prices were effectively at their minimum, it might be as accurate to date the end of the rise of real wages at

1899. Wholesale prices at least rose rapidly during the South African War, and it is doubtful what is the correct measurement for real wages from 1898 to 1902. There seems to be no doubt that, except for the years of the brief crisis of 1907, there was no significant change in real wages in the thirteen years before the Great War. The full examination of the causes which led to this change of tendency, from generally rising real wages for the great part of the second half of the nineteenth century to stationariness in the twentieth, calls for more research than it has received. It should be added that if we had not allowed for some shifting of occupation towards higher wages, we should have found a definite fall in real wages after 1902.

It is argued in Chapter VI that the income per head of the whole population followed nearly the same course as money wage-rates, throughout the thirty-five years, and when allowance is made for the changes of prices the same general movements are found in both the main sections of the National Income.

No estimates are here attempted for the years *between* 1914 and 1924. The course of wages and prices from 1914 to 1921 is discussed elsewhere (ref. 51). A great deal of doubt must remain about the movements of average wages and the actual cost of living, though there is copious detail for many of the items. A very serious attempt, however, has been made to find the net result of all the changes from 1911 or 1914 to 1924, a year in which conditions were temporarily stable. It is found that average money earnings for those in full work had increased about 94 per cent., and that the gain in real wages was about 10 per cent. At the same time hours of work had generally been decreased by some 10 per cent. This increase was partly at the expense of income from property, for the whole national income per head is estimated to have risen no faster than prices—not so fast if the diminution of income from abroad is taken into account. But this statement depends to some extent on what definition of income is used, and it is explained in Chapter VI.

After 1924 prices fell rapidly to a minimum in 1933, and then took an upward turn, which has continued to the date of writing (1937). Money wages began to fall later, from 1926, and fell much more slowly than prices, so that real wages rose some 18 per cent. on the average—the exact rise is a matter of conjecture or even of definition, because, as discussed in Chapter II, the measurement of purchasing power by the cost of living index-number has become less satisfactory as real average wages have increased. Since 1933 the increase of money wages appears to have lagged behind that of prices. It has generally been the case, as indeed we should expect *a priori*, that real wages fall for some time when prices rise and rise when prices fall. The stationariness of money wages is no new phenomenon. These tendencies are modified if we take unemployment into account, for that rises after a crisis when prices break, and falls when prices recover.

The division of income into the classes 'arising from property' and 'arising from employment' has considerable importance, but it is blurred by the existence of income from direct work for gain—'working on own account'—which may contain a small or large constituent properly attributable to property, small in the case of an itinerant knife-grinder, large when a firm operates on its own capital. On the other hand, the division of income from employment into wages and salaries is artificial if it merely depends on the method or contract of payment, and is a matter of delimitation rather than of principle if it depends on occupation. It is certainly not reasonable to regard wage-earners as producing the wealth of the nation, and all other classes as parasitic, as is sometimes implied. But the manual working class is sufficiently distinct even now to have characteristics of its own, and has a certain class consciousness, and the proportion that wages form of the total national income has often been the subject of estimate. This proportion is estimated from various points of view in Chapter VI. When the same items are included, and we deal throughout with aggregate income, or with home-produced income, or with social income, in the phraseology of that chapter, it is remarkable that we get very nearly the same percentage, 40 to 43, according to the definition of income, from 1880, or even from 1860, to 1935.[1] There have been temporary variations of two or three points up or down, and the direction of such small changes has sometimes depended on which definition of income we take, but it appears to be impossible to establish the existence of any permanent tendency to alter the proportion.

This approximate constancy is the more remarkable in view of the fact that the manual-labour class has formed a proportion of the occupied population that has diminished since 1880; according to the classification used in the text it was 80 per cent. in 1880, 74 per cent. in 1911, and 72 per cent. in 1931. The smaller relative numbers have obtained the same relative amount.

The increasing number of persons engaged in clerical, professional and other middle-class occupations is analysed in Appendix E, pp. 127–36. The proportion of men so employed increased moderately from 1881 to 1911, and has since then remained nearly stationary. The proportion of occupied women and girls in such occupations increased rapidly throughout the period, and especially between 1911 and 1921, when the entries to domestic service fell off, and the number of typists, clerks and shop assistants became much greater.

When we are considering the progress of the working class we should have regard to the fact that, especially since the introduction of compulsory education, there has been a transfer of the more intelligent, at least in book knowledge, from manual labour to clerical work, teaching and other professional occupations. The existing middle class must be very largely recruited from the children of working-class parents or grandparents. In fact, the recent London and other town Surveys have shown that in households in which the head is an artisan, or even labourer, the children are frequently typists, clerks, shop

[1] Mr Clark, with a different definition, obtains a different percentage, but, over the period from 1924 which his studies cover, constancy is still marked (ref. 70).

assistants or teachers, while others follow their father's occupation. Especially among young women there is an increase of earnings with each grade of education; for men the wages of skilled workmen overlap the smaller salaries. It is not practical or reasonable to construct an average of the earnings of workmen fifty years ago, and compare it with the average of wages and salaries of their descendants now; no doubt the latter average would be raised above that of wages alone, but not very significantly. But together with any statement of the change (or constancy) of the proportion that wages form of the national income, we should have figures showing the synchronous increase in the number of at least the lower range of salaries. The structure of commerce and industry has altered in the direction of more administration in relation to manual work.

Though it is not practical to give a series in which wages are combined with small salaries, it is attempted to trace the relation between earned income as a whole and income from property. Such estimates are discussed in Chapter VI. The data are rather unsatisfactory, and there is a permanent difficulty, as named above, in defining or measuring earnings of those who use their own capital. The general result is that on any constant definition and method this proportion has changed very little. It is of course not possible that the wage proportion should be constant, and the property proportion also constant, while the salary proportion increased. But the variations, as shown, for example, in Table XV, p. 99, have usually been slow, and the changes tend to be submerged in the difficulties of classification.

All such problems have become increasingly difficult to handle because of the enhanced amount taken by taxes and rates, for interest on the national debt and for social services. The income received is not all available for free expenditure. Interest is largely a transfer from one group of taxpayers to another. Of the sums devoted to social services some are direct transfers, as for example non-contributory old-age pensions, some are for common public purposes, some are for the relief of want or sickness, some are subsidies to selected industries.

Even if the final incidence of taxes and rates could be traced, it would still not be possible to allot a particular tax or rate to a particular service, for all taxes are pooled in the Public Accounts, and a considerable amount of the receipts of taxation is transferred to the aid of rates, or shares expenses with rates. We cannot reasonably say, for example, that receipts from income-tax, sur-tax, and estate duties are allotted to debt-interest and defence, because in 1935–6 the first total is nearly equal to the second, while the receipts from beer, tea, sugar, entertainments and tobacco pay for expenditure under the heading 'Health, Labour and Insurance', while the customs and excise on spirits meet three-quarters of central expenditure on education. All that can be done from the point of view of avoidance of duplication in national income estimates is to show the relevant statistics, and work out any proportions on different reasonable hypotheses. These questions of definition are not discussed in this book, and only those statistics of transfers are used which are included in the studies from which the estimates are drawn.

The increase in real wages has at no time in the past forty years been rapid. Up to the date of the war there had been no progress for fifteen or twenty years. Over the war period the increase in the average money wage would have been no greater than the rise of prices, if there had not been a shifting of occupations and methods of payment. Since 1924 the rather considerable rise has been because prices have fallen faster than wages. These movements are not enough to account for the progress that is evident to any one who has observed the wage-earning classes during the period. The development of social expenditure, whatever the source of the money, has through old-age pensions and the many insurance services been an enormous help in preserving the standard of life attained by any family; the special increase in the lower rates of wages has levelled up these standards. There has in forty years been a great advance of knowledge, as the younger generations have matured in an environment of more general education. The reduction of the hours of work in 1919–20 has had far-reaching effects. To this should be added the reduction of stringency in making the income meet necessary expenses, due to the smaller number of children in almost every section of society. Unfortunately this amelioration is not to be found in those districts and industries where unemployment has been prolonged and wage progress has not been uniform, so that some groups have had exceptional good fortune, while others have barely preserved their standard. Since this book is limited to measurable aspects of change and principally to general averages, it does not afford the material for the description or complete study of the changing 'condition of the people'. It may, however, serve as a companion to the numerous local Surveys which are now available, and provide some historical background for modern investigators.

# Chapter I

## THE COURSE OF AVERAGE WAGES

The main purpose of this chapter is to estimate the changes in average wages of the working class of the United Kingdom during the period 1880–1936, with some reference to earlier dates, together with summary figures for particular industries.

From the workman's point of view it is the amount of money that he receives for a week's work that is the important thing, and it is this we have in mind rather than the change to the employer in the cost of a given quantity of work. Some statistics of the number of hours that constituted a normal week from time to time are given on pp. 25–6 below.

It is not only natural, but necessitated by the data, that we study first the wages for the normal week and deal subsequently with the effects of unemployment, over- or short-time, holidays and time lost owing to sickness. Also we must at first ignore the compulsory reductions for health and unemployment insurance, though these should be taken into account when we consider the adequacy of wages in relation to standards of expenditure. The problem of the varying purchasing power of money is discussed in the next chapter.

A distinction is sometimes made between wages and earnings; the wage is taken to be the contractual time-rate, while earnings are either the receipts from piece-work or the actual amount received in the week allowing for over- or short-time. Our first aim is to measure the changes in the week's earnings, as they would be if exactly the normal time was worked, whatever the basis of payment.

## I. 1880–1914

In the earlier part of our period the main material consists of time-rates, and up to the present date these remain the principal sources of current information. But the Wage Censuses, especially since the war, depend primarily on records of earnings, so that we have to devise a means of connecting the changes of rates with those of earnings.

Since statements of wages for any one date depend partly on the definition adopted and partly on the bias of their source, so that we get different accounts from trade unions and from employers, each correct according to the facts used, I have adopted from the first of my published studies, that in 1895 (ref. 1), the plan of using only those accounts which relate to more than one date and are compiled on a uniform method. Variation from the ideal definition may be expected to be of nearly the same relative amount at each date, so that the ratio found is more accurate than the statement for any one date. In the earlier decades, however, even these ratios must be used with care and collated with other sources when possible, for the trade-union rates, for example, may have been at one time an ideal aimed at but not universally reached, and at another a minimum that was below the average paid to all the workmen concerned. The principal corrective source is found in successive Wage Censuses.

Thus the general plan has been to assemble series of the time-rates from Trade-Union Reports or those of the Labour Department of the Board of Trade, later the Ministry of Labour, and from employers' accounts of earnings, and series of piece-rates. The results, averaged so as to take into account the changing relative importance of the occupations, give dead reckonings over series of years between one Census and the next; the Censuses afford more perfect observations, by which the dead reckonings can be rectified.

To pass from a series of time- or piece-rates to the movement of earnings we have to take into account several factors. First, a change of piece-rates is seldom exactly proportional to the resulting change of earnings. A workman, aiming at a customary weekly wage packet, may work harder or longer in face of a reduction, or ease off when there is an increase. When an increase is given in compensation for a reduction of hours in the recognised week, it has been found[1] that earnings have increased. In some cases reductions of piece-rates are agreed upon because the machinery has improved so that more can be produced for the same effort; in order to get willing work the employers make only such a reduction as will leave some advantage to the operative, so that a reduction of piece-rates leads to an increase of earnings.

Secondly, especially in the latter part of our period, there are various systems of bonus on production and other additions to a minimum time-rate. There are also modifications for normal night work or over-time, where these are essential to the occupation.

Thirdly, there is a continual shifting of the relative numbers within an industry engaged on pure time-rates or pure piece-rates, or some combination of the two, and also between occupations. In particular, as machinery developed, relatively fewer unskilled workers were necessary and more machine-minders, with possible changes in the relative numbers of fully skilled men. A considerable part of our information at the Census dates relates to industries as a whole, and the average for the industry may move at a different rate from that shown by the average of the series of wage changes. In the investigations on the earnings of engineers, shipbuilders and cotton operatives (refs. 11, 12, 13, 14, 15, 87) these changes have been brought into the resulting index-numbers, and the same has been possible for coal over the years that include the war; but in general the corrections can only be made at the date of a Census.

Fourthly, when we are considering the general average for all occupations, we have to take into account the changes in the relative numbers employed in the different industries, such as the increase in mining and the diminution of agriculture and the fall in the number of domestic servants. A minor factor is the change in the relative number of adults and juveniles and the

---

[1] For illustrations of such changes the statistics of earnings in the cotton industry should be studied.

disappearance of half-timers. For these changes we have to
depend primarily on the Population Censuses (Occupation
Tables), supplemented in more recent times by the statistics
resulting from the Unemployment Insurance Scheme.

This leads to two different conceptions of wage changes, or a
division of the causes of change into two groups. One is the
movement due to changes in wage-rates, the other the shifting
of the relative numbers in occupations, normally towards
higher or rising wages, which makes the increase of the general
average greater than that of the average of the occupational or
industrial series. It is fortunately possible at several dates to
separate these factors by a method explained in Appendix B.
We return to this subject below.

It is clear that a minute study of the material, which is of
many different kinds, is necessary before any generalisation can
be reached. In the end a great deal depends on personal
judgment of the validity, appropriateness and accuracy of the
data. No exact statistical justification can be shown for the
details included, and the elaboration of formulae does not re-
move the elements of approximation in the data. Fortunately
there have been two nearly independent estimates for the
period up to 1914 (ref. 49, p. 165 and ref. 86), and again for the
period 1924 to 1935, and in each case they are in close agreement with each other.

The principal series which shows the estimated movement of
the general average has not hitherto been published *in extenso*
with full explanation of the method followed, backed by detailed statistics of the constituents. As one industry after another
has been studied and as information has accumulated owing to
the publication of a Census or from other sources, the series
first put forward has been modified. Many of the results have
been published from time to time, but some have only been
given in unpublished lectures. The preliminary material is to
be found, some of it in a stage already partly worked up, in the
books and articles listed below (pp. 142 *seq.*); but it would not be
possible for a reader of those to work out completely by any

formula the final series. The material is too extensive to print in full, and the compilation of the final series with the various adjustments of weights used is too complicated for exhibition in a simple form.

Table I gives the results of the process now described. The first column of index-numbers gives my final estimate of the course of average earnings for a normal week of all wage-earners in the United Kingdom, the changes in the relative numbers in different occupations and industries being taken into account. The principal check on its accuracy is found from the Reports of the Wage Censuses of 1886 and 1906 (see Appendix A). For adult males the average earnings of those included in the Reports were 24s. 7d. in 1886 and 30s. 9d. in 1906; the increase is thus 24 per cent. When allowance is made for the change of the industries included and for the earnings of women, boys and girls, we get the 26 per cent. increase given by the table. From 1880 to 1886 there had been very little movement. After 1906 there was an immediate rise, a fall and a further rise. Up to 1911 I made a further detailed estimate (ref. 45); from 1911 to 1914 dependence has been on the re-corded changes of wage-rates only, and in fact it is unlikely that there was any important change in the factors not taken into account. For changes in numbers the 1921 Population Census was ultimately used in comparison with that of 1911 to bridge the war period. Mr G. H. Wood made in 1909 (ref. 86) an independent estimate for the period 1850 to 1902, and has communicated to me an unpublished continuation to include 1910. His results are given in the second column of index-numbers in the table. It is seen that the only essential difference between the first two columns of index-numbers is from 1887 to 1891; this is traceable mainly to a different estimate of the effect of a considerable rise in miners' earnings. This illustrates the difficulty of making exact calculations. In retrospect the discrepancy is not serious.

The third column is based on statistics in the *Eighteenth*

## TABLE I

*General Wage and Earnings Index-numbers, 1880–1914*

| Year | Allowing for change in numbers in occupations | | Not allowing for change in numbers in occupations | |
|---|---|---|---|---|
| | Bowley | Wood | Labour Department | Wood |
| | 1 | 2 | 3 | 4 |
| 1880 | 100 | 100 | 100 | 100 |
| 1881 | 100 | 100 | 102 | 100 |
| 1882 | 103 | 100 | 103 | 100 |
| 1883 | 103 | 101 | 103 | 101 |
| 1884 | 103 | 102 | 102 | 101 |
| 1885 | 101 | 101 | 101 | 100 |
| 1886 | 100 | 101 | 100 | 99 |
| 1887 | 101 | 101 | 100 | 100 |
| 1888 | 104 | 103 | 102 | 100 |
| 1889 | 110 | 106 | 105 | 103 |
| 1890 | 114 | 111 | 109 | 108 |
| 1891 | 115 | 111 | 110 | 108 |
| 1892 | 115 | 110 | 109 | 107 |
| 1893 | 115 | 110 | 109 | 106 |
| 1894 | 115 | 110 | 108 | 106 |
| 1895 | 115 | 110 | 107 | 105 |
| 1896 | 115 | 111 | 109 | 106 |
| 1897 | 116 | 113 | 110 | 107 |
| 1898 | 120 | 114 | 112 | 109 |
| 1899 | 123 | 117 | 115 | 111 |
| 1900 | 130 | 122 | 120 | 116 |
| 1901 | 128 | 122 | 119 | 115 |
| 1902 | 126 | 120 | 118 | 115 |
| 1903 | 125 | 120 | 117 | 114 |
| 1904 | 123 | 120 | 116 | 113 |
| 1905 | 123 | 119 | 117 | 112 |
| 1906 | 126 | 123 | 119 | 115 |
| 1907 | 133 | 129 | 123 | 115 |
| 1908 | 130 | 127 | 122 | 115 |
| 1909 | 129 | 125 | 121 | 115 |
| 1910 | 130 | 127 | 121 | 115 |
| 1911 | 131 | — | 122 | — |
| 1912 | 135 | — | 125 | — |
| 1913 | 137 | — | 129 | — |
| 1914 | 138 | — | 130 | — |

*Abstract of Labour Statistics*, p. 120. It is the unweighted average of five series, viz. building, mean of rates of wages for carpenters, bricklayers and masons in large towns; coal, weighted percentage changes in rates in the principal districts; engineering, average of trade-union rates for fitters, turners, patternmakers and ironmoulders in a small number of large towns; textiles, weighted changes in piece-rates in cotton, linen and jute without any reference to wool; agriculture, average cash rates of ordinary labourers in 183 farms in England, Wales and Scotland, and of earnings of married horsemen in Scotland. This list shows that dependence has been on data readily obtainable, mainly of skilled operatives in the first three groups. There is no attempt to allow for change in relative numbers either within or between industries, and the five groups are taken as of equal importance. The series can only give a guide to dates of change and movements over short periods.

The fourth column is also due to Mr Wood (*loc. cit.*). He terms the series 'Money Wages for Workmen of unchanged grade'. It appears to be obtained by taking the same data as for column 2, and applying fixed weights instead of allowing for the varying rates of growth of different occupations. This reckoning is of importance, not only as indicating, when taken with column 2, the effect of these changes, but also because for the individual workman the thing that is interesting is the change in his wages, not a general average affecting the next generation.

There is no doubt about the general movement of money wages during the thirty-four years. After little movement from 1880 to 1886, there was a marked rise till 1891. For the next five years rates fell slightly, but the general average for all was stationary. From 1896 to 1900 there was a rapid increase, due largely to miners' wages, but the maximum of 1900 was not preserved and there was a recession till 1904 or 1905. Then progress was resumed till 1914, with a check in 1908–9.

This movement of the average is the resultant of very unequal changes in different occupations and industries, some of which are shown in the next table. There columns 3, 4 and 5

## TABLE II

*Index-numbers for Separate Industries. Wages or Earnings, 1880–1914*

| Year | Agri-culture | Coal | Build-ing | Engin-eering and ship-building | Cotton | Wool | Printers |
|------|------|------|------|------|------|------|------|
| | 1 | 2 | 3 | 4 | 5 | 6 | 7 |
| 1880 | 100 | 100 | 100 | 100 | 100 | 100 | 100 |
| 1881 | 99 | 103 | 100 | 99 | 103 | — | — |
| 1882 | 97 | 110 | 100 | 97 | 103 | — | — |
| 1883 | 96 | 112 | 100 | 96 | 105 | 95 | 97 |
| 1884 | 94 | 107 | 100 | 94 | 105 | — | — |
| 1885 | 93 | 103 | 100 | 93 | 103 | — | — |
| 1886 | 91 | 99 | 100 | 91 | 102 | 91 | 98 |
| 1887 | 94 | 99 | 101 | 94 | 104 | — | — |
| 1888 | 96 | 105 | 101 | 96 | 108 | — | — |
| 1889 | 97 | 123 | 103 | 97 | 109 | — | — |
| 1890 | 100 | 140 | 104 | 100 | 110 | — | — |
| 1891 | 100 | 141 | 104 | 100 | 115 | — | — |
| 1892 | 100 | 128 | 105 | 100 | 116 | — | — |
| 1893 | 99 | 131 | 107 | 99 | 116 | — | 101 |
| 1894 | 99 | 124 | 107 | 99 | 116 | — | 101 |
| 1895 | 97 | 118 | 108 | 97 | 116 | — | — |
| 1896 | 97 | 117 | 109 | 97 | 117 | — | — |
| 1897 | 99 | 118 | 111 | 99 | 117 | — | 102 |
| 1898 | 101 | 128 | 112 | 101 | 119 | — | 102 |
| 1899 | 103 | 136 | 113 | 103 | 120 | — | 102 |
| 1900 | 109 | 163 | 115 | 109 | 123 | — | — |
| 1901 | 110 | 153 | 115 | 110 | 124 | 91 | — |
| 1902 | 110 | 142 | 115 | 110 | 123 | — | — |
| 1903 | 110 | 138 | 115 | 110 | 123 | — | — |
| 1904 | 110 | 134 | 115 | 110 | 124 | — | — |
| 1905 | 110 | 132 | 115 | 110 | 127 | — | — |
| 1906 | 110 | 136 | 115 | 110 | 132 | — | — |
| 1907 | 110 | 157 | 115 | 110 | — | — | — |
| 1908 | 110 | 152 | 115 | 110 | — | — | — |
| 1909 | 110 | 145 | 115 | 110 | — | — | — |
| 1910 | 110 | 146 | 115 | 110 | — | — | — |
| 1911 | 112 | 144 | 115 | 112 | — | — | — |
| 1912 | 114 | 152 | 116 | 114 | — | — | — |
| 1913 | 118 | 163 | 119 | 118 | — | — | — |
| 1914 | 122 | 160 | 123 | 122 | — | — | — |

come from the elaborate studies in the *Statistical Journal* (refs. 7, 8, 9, 86), brought up-to-date as far as possible. These relate to the averages for all persons in the industries and the changing importance of the occupations. Column 2, on the other hand, is simply that from the *Labour Abstract*, and relates to piece-rates with no reference to any other factors. For Agriculture, column 1, the figures till 1895 are based on the study in the *Statistical Journal* (refs. 2, 3, 4, 5). They differ from those in the *Labour Abstract* in that there rates are estimated to be nearly stationary year by year from 1880 to 1891, whereas there is sufficient evidence that there was a considerable fall and rise in a number of counties. There is always great difficulty in making an adequate estimate of average earnings in agriculture, and for the years subsequent to 1895 there is no certainty of the exact movement. There is no doubt, however, that substantial increases took place between 1896 and 1901, and after 1910.

For Wool and Worsted, Mr Wood's estimates (ref. 88) differ substantially from those given here, column 6; the fact is that the changes were very different as between Bradford, Leeds, Huddersfield and Dewsbury; the information is insufficient, partly owing to the many different industries contained in wool and worsted combing, spinning and manufacture, and it has never proved possible to trace far back the numerical history of earnings in this group. It is quite possible that the figure for 1901 ought to be raised; in any case there was a rise by the Census date 1906.

The fragmentary entries for Printers, column 7 (ref. 6), only relate to time-rates for compositors, which do not measure the movement of earnings. They are included as an illustration of the stationariness of some time-rates over long periods, a phenomenon which Mr Wood has examined in the *Economic Journal*, 1901, pp. 151 *seq.* (ref. 89). As a further illustration details may be given of the London Bricklayer and his Labourer from 1861 to 1914. These have a special interest as being the rates paid for work the nature of which hardly changed in the period.

| Year | Hourly rates in London | | Hours in full summer week |
|---|---|---|---|
| | Bricklayer | Labourer | |
| | $d$. | $d$. | |
| 1861 to 1864 | 7 | $4\frac{1}{4}$ | $56\frac{1}{2}$ |
| 1865 | $7\frac{1}{2}$ | $4\frac{1}{2}$ | ,, |
| 1866 | 8 | $4\frac{1}{2}$ | ,, |
| 1867 | 8 | $4\frac{3}{4}$ | ,, |
| 1872 | $8\frac{1}{2}$ | $5\frac{1}{4}$ | ,, |
| 1873 to 1887 | 9 | $5\frac{3}{4}$ | $52\frac{1}{2}$ |
| 1888 to 1892 | 9 | 6 | ,, |
| 1893 to 1895 | $9\frac{1}{2}$ | $6\frac{1}{2}$ | 50 |
| 1896 | 10 | $6\frac{1}{2}$ | ,, |
| 1897 to 1899 | 10 | 7 | ,, |
| 1900 to 1913 | $10\frac{1}{2}$ | 7 | ,, |
| 1914 | $11\frac{1}{2}$ | 8 | ,, |

The bricklayer's wage was unchanged from 1873 to 1892, and again from 1900 to 1913. The increases in 1873 and in 1893 were to compensate for the reduction of hours. The summer week's rates were in 1872 40s. 0¼d., in 1873 39s. 4½d. and in 1893 39s. 7d., after the increases in hourly rates at the last two dates.

## II. 1860–1880

Prior to 1880 there is only enough information to follow the changes in different trades and to give a very general account of the movement of the average, so that the following numbers are only indicative, not exact measurements.

*General Movement of Average Wages, 1860 to 1880*

| Year | Bowley | Wood |
|---|---|---|
| 1860 | 81 | 78 |
| 1866 | 91 | 90 |
| 1870 | 91 | 91 |
| 1874 | 111 | 106 |
| 1877 | 106 | 103 |
| 1880 | 100 | 100 |

In each case the average wages are given as a percentage of the 1880 level; the first was published in 1895 (ref. 1), the second in 1909 (ref. 86). They agree in the dates, but not in the amount of change. There was a rise in 1860–6, and a very rapid and unevenly distributed rise in 1870–4, followed by a considerable fall.

Thus the year 1880, taken as the starting-point of our main study, shows the position reached after the reaction that followed the great crisis of 1873–4. It has been seen that it initiated a period of generally stationary wage-rates.

With this study of money rates it is necessary to take into account the changes in the purchasing power of wages, as in Chapter II below. It will then be seen that we have so far only one of the two factors that determine real wages, and that the introduction of the other factor gives a greatly modified impression of the nature and dates of movement.

## III. 1914–1924

It is convenient to take as fixed points the years 1914 and 1924. For 1914 we can safely assume that there were no important deviations from the reckoning we get from ordinary sources to carry on from the Wage Census of 1906 and the Population Census of 1911. In 1924 we have again a Wage Census. Between these dates there were the great changes in wages and in numbers in industries during the war, the enormous rise in money wages up to the end of 1921 or later, and their subsequent collapse.

Considerable detail of the course of wages from 1914 till two years after the Armistice is to be found in my *Prices and Wages in the United Kingdom, 1914 to 1920* (ref. 51), and there is no need to repeat that part of the analysis which related only to transitory movements. The factors whose effect was lasting were the increase in piece-rate and bonus systems, the different rates of change for skilled and unskilled labour, a specially rapid increase in the wages of some women, and a considerable change in the relative importance of industries. We may consider the last factor first with the help of the 1921 Population Census. By that date demobilisation was practically complete, and many women who had undertaken special war work had retired from gainful occupations, while those who would normally have been occupied, but had gone into munition

TABLE III

*Relative numbers occupied in Industrial Groups in England and Wales, 1911 and 1921*

Per 1000 of all occupied, males and females separately

|  | Males | | Females | |
|---|---|---|---|---|
|  | 1911 | 1921 | 1911 | 1921 |
| Agriculture | 99 | 86 | 20 | 17 |
| Coal | 85 | 93 | 0 | 0 |
| Bricks, pottery, cement, quarries, glass, etc. | 25 | 23 | 8 | 11 |
| Chemicals | 9 | 12 | 5 | 10 |
| Metals, engineering, vehicles, metal products | 124 | 157 | 21 | 44 |
| Textiles | 45 | 40 | 136 | 129 |
| Clothing | 30 | 26 | 145 | 99 |
| Food, drink, tobacco | 28 | 28 | 31 | 39 |
| Paper, printing | 17 | 18 | 20 | 23 |
| Wood, furniture | 19 | 17 | 5 | 5 |
| Building, public works | 75 | 62 | 0 | 2 |
| Other manufactures | 18 | 18 | 16 | 23 |
| Gas, water, electricity | 10 | 13 | 0 | 1 |
| Transport | 97 | 96 | 4 | 8 |
| Finance, commerce, dealing | 144 | 127 | 96 | 147 |
| National and Local Government. Defence | 55 | 76 | 16 | 38 |
| Professions, entertainments | 33 | 34 | 77 | 90 |
| Personal service | 52 | 43 | 386 | 298 |
| Miscellaneous | 35 | 31 | 14 | 16 |
| Total | 1000 | 1000 | 1000 | 1000 |
| Numbers occupied | 11,454 | 12,113 | 4832 | 5065 |

More than half of the women under the heading 'Professions' were teachers.

factories during the war, had settled down in some cases in their normal work, in others in occupations which had become increasingly open to them, such as clerical work and some branches of engineering. Actually a smaller proportion of the female population was classed as occupied in the 1921 Census than ten years before, the diminution being found among married women and widows. Of those occupied, a much smaller number were domestic servants, many more were typists, clerks or shop assistants, and the numbers in metal and some other manufactures had increased. Other changes are shown in Table III opposite. Among men there was an increase in mining and in the metal trades, a fall in the number of builders, and an increase in Government service which compensated for their replacement by women in clerical work.

Though these changes were of considerable magnitude, their effect on average wages was by 1924 extremely slight, as is seen on p. 110 below. The main reasons for this unexpected result were that the influx into coal-mining proved to be into an industry where wages rose less than the average, while women did not earn more in some of the occupations in which their numbers increased than they would have received in domestic service.

The necessary estimates for further changes in numbers between 1921 and 1924 were made with the help of the statistics of unemployment insurance.

Two illustrations may be given of the relation of changes in earnings to changes in nominal rates.

In Volume II of the *Reports of the Committee on Industry and Trade*, 'Further Factors in Industrial and Commercial Efficiency', pp. 92–3, there is a table that shows the changes in Wage-Rates and Weekly Earnings between 1914 and 1925, from which the following has been compiled.

*Engineering Industries. Wages and Earnings in 1925 expressed as percentages of the levels in 1914*

|  | Fitters | Labourers | All operatives |
|---|---|---|---|
| Time-rates | 145 | 176 | 160 |
| Time-earnings | 156 | 185 | 171 |
| Payment by results | 164 | 198 | 175 |
| Together | — | — | 178 |

Here, while time-rates increased 60 per cent., average earnings of all increased 78 per cent.—more than in any one category, because the higher earning groups increased in numbers more rapidly than the lower.

There was a general reduction of weekly hours of work throughout industry in 1919, so that the hourly rates increased more than the weekly rates with which we are here dealing. Usually the same week's time-rate was paid after the change as before, and piece-rates were raised in proportion to the reduction ratio of hours. Thus, in the cotton industry, hours were reduced from $55\frac{1}{2}$ to 48 in July 1919; before the change piece-rates were at 215, compared with 105 in 1914; after it at 245, from which a little arithmetic shows that the rate per hour, assuming the same output, was reduced $1\frac{1}{2}$ per cent. Actual weekly earnings were, however, greater after the reduction of hours, and with no further increase in rates showed an increase of 20 per cent. from April 1919 to April 1920 (ref. 51, p. 178).

In the whole period 1914 to 1925 piece-rates for cotton weavers and spinners increased 86 per cent., or, making full allowance for the reduction of hours, nominally 61 per cent. for the week; according to the above-named Report earnings had increased 85 or 90 per cent. Thus the reduction in hours was followed by such increased hourly output as to make the week's output the same as before.

The *Abstract of Labour Statistics*, 1927, pp. 118–19, gives a general average of the changes in time- and piece-rates from 1914 to 1925. For 1924 the increase over 1914 is given as 70 or 75 per cent., raised by December 1925 to the full 75 per cent. But a careful study of other information, such as the Report quoted above and the Wage Census of 1924, leads to an estimate of 94 per cent. for the change in average earnings for all occupied, taking into account all known factors. The increase per hour's work may be estimated at about 115 per cent. Thus 100 + 94 per cent. is the number adopted in the sequel for the general index-number of average earnings in a normal week's work.

In the little table on p. 13 of engineers' earnings it will be noticed that unskilled workmen had benefited more than skilled. Such a difference is found generally; it arose from the procedure early in the war of giving the same flat increase to all grades to compensate for the increased cost of food; these war bonuses were first regarded as temporary measures to meet a situation which was not expected to last. The effect on wages can be seen from a continuation of the table of wages in the London building industry.

*London Builders*

| Year | Bricklayer | | | | Labourer | | | |
|---|---|---|---|---|---|---|---|---|
| | Rate per hour | | Rate for full summer week | | Rate per hour | | Rate for full summer week | |
| | d. | % | s. | % | d. | % | s. | % |
| 1914 | 11½ | 100 | 47·9 | 100 | 8 | 100 | 33·3 | 100 |
| 1919 | 21 | 182 | 87·5 | 182 | 17 | 213 | 70·9 | 213 |
| 1920 | 28 | 243 | 102·7 | 214 | 25 | 312 | 91·7 | 275 |
| 1925 | 21½ | 187 | 78·8 | 165 | 16½ | 206 | 60·5 | 181 |
| 1933 | 19 | 165 | 69·8 | 145 | 14¼ | 178 | 52·2 | 157 |
| 1936 | 20 | 174 | 73·3 | 153 | 15 | 175 | 55·0 | 165 |

In 1914 summer hours were 50 per week. Between the dates of the entries for 1919 and 1920 they were reduced to 44.

Rates rose by a series of steps from 1915 to the maximum shown in 1920. Then they were reduced gradually, with reference to the cost of living index, to a minimum in 1933. They rose in 1935 and 1936 to the level shown.

It will be noticed that from 1914 to 1925 the bricklayer's hourly rate increased by 16½d., the labourer's by 17d., so that from being 70 per cent. of the bricklayer's it became 89 per cent. This was recognised as anomalous, and subsequently it was agreed that the labourer's rate should be as near as possible three-quarters of the bricklayer's.

The wages of women rose more rapidly than those of men during the period 1914 to 1924 taken as a whole. A considerable proportion of women employees are in occupations for which minimum rates are prescribed under Trade Boards, and the increases in these up to the maximum in 1920 were generally more favourable to women than they were to men in occupations in general.

A close study of the Wage Censuses of 1906 and 1924 indicates that while the average earnings in industry of males increased 100 per cent. in those eighteen years those of females increased 127 per cent.; and that while the females' average was 43 per cent. of the males' in 1906 it was 48 per cent. in 1924. The latter Census does not separate boys from men or girls from women, but very roughly it may be said that the average for adult men in industry (mining and agriculture excluded) was 29s. to 30s. weekly in 1906, and was near 60s. in 1924, while for adult women the corresponding figures were 12s. 6d. and 29s. Since the 1906 Census omitted out-workers and other low-paid women who have since benefited by the Trade Boards' minima, the increase is probably under-estimated.

A more definite comparison can be made from the estimate on the next page of the general change from 1914 to 1924. There it appears that the average weekly earnings of all male manual workers increased 91 per cent., while those of females increased 112 per cent.

In general the course of women's wages has been parallel to that of unskilled men, who, as we have seen, have obtained a greater rise than have skilled.

Many writers have found a distinction between the increases of wages in so-called sheltered and unsheltered trades. This appears to be a too hasty generalisation. Among industries working for export wages in many cases had increased as much as had the average; prices of exports rose enormously after the war. On the other hand, where production for home use was faced with competition from abroad wage increases over the ten years were in some industries below the average. Wages paid by Local Authorities increased greatly, but this is largely due to the fact that most of the men are unskilled. The principal industries in which the increase was relatively low were agriculture, coal-mining and general engineering. The variations in the rates of increase are to be found rather by a study of the circumstances of the particular industries than by any general hypothesis.

The table that follows affords a general view of the movement of average earnings. In it the figures printed in italics are not the result of complete information, but are on the assumption that the increases are similar to those in selected industries for which the data are sufficient, with reference also to sporadic records of wages.

### TABLE IV

*Increase in Average Weekly Earnings, 1914 to 1924*

United Kingdom[1]

| | Percentage increase | |
|---|---|---|
| | Males | Females |
| Coal | 63 | — |
| Other mining and quarrying | 63 | — |
| Iron, steel, engineering, vehicles, metal work | 87 | 126 |
| Cotton | 92 | 87 |
| Wool and Worsted | 140 | 136 |
| Bleaching, etc. | 106 | 120 |
| Other textiles | 124 | — |
| Pottery, china, bricks, chemicals | 111 | 130 |
| Boots | 125 | 173 |
| Other clothing | 111 | 130 |
| Leather, furs | 97 | — |
| Food, tobacco | 97 | 108 |
| Paper | 123 | 145 |
| Printing | 147 | — |
| Wood, furniture | 103 | — |
| Building, construction | 95 | — |
| Other manufactures | 97 | 108 |
| Agriculture | 68 | — |
| Transport | 101 | — |
| Public Utilities | 105 | — |
| Personal Services | 97 | 108 |
| Other occupations | 97 | 108 |
| Together | 90·6 | 112 |
| | 94·3 | |

[1] Based on p. 37 of *The National Income*, 1924 (47).

When the increases for males are combined with those for females, with due allowance for changes in their relative numbers, it is computed that the increase of the average wage per head for all manual labour from 1914 to 1924 was 94 per cent.

## IV. 1924–1937

Average wages were nearly stationary from 1924 to the end of 1929 according to the index of the London and Cambridge Economic Service, and then there was a fall to a minimum in 1933–4 and an increase to 1936 and later. Mr Ramsbottom's index (ref. 80), which takes in more industries and in different proportions, shows a reduction in 1927 and 1928. Both series indicate a trifling rise to 1926 and a slow fall to 1933, and the last entry in Mr Ramsbottom's series differs very little from that of the Economic Service at the same date, so that they agree in showing a reduction of 6 per cent. from 1924 to 1935.

Neither of the series makes any allowance for change in the relative numbers in occupations, or for the possible difference between the movements of earnings and rates. This is discussed in Appendices A and B. There seems to be no significant difference between the reckoning by wage-rates with fixed numbers in the industries and that by earnings after allowance for all disturbing factors when 1928 or 1931 is compared with 1924. But the Wage Census of 1935, together with the statistics of insured persons at work, shows a gain of about 3 per cent. of earnings over rates due to a multiplicity of causes. The main reason for this excess appears to be simply increased earnings by piece-work or over-time when trade improved after 1933. Hence the best approximation is to use the index-numbers as first stated from 1924 to 1933 inclusive, and to raise them to 96 in 1934 and to 98 in 1935. The records of earnings available for some industries in 1936 indicate that the same process has continued, and the number 100 is suggested for that year. Rates increased further by about 2 per cent. on the average in the first half of 1937, but it is not necessary to estimate for that year.

The series of index-numbers in Tables I and V are combined in Table VII in the next chapter, p. 30. The net result

## TABLE V

*Course of Wages,* 1924 *to* 1937

United Kingdom

| Date | Index-numbers | |
|---|---|---|
| | Economic Service | Mr Ramsbottom's |
| 1924 December | 100 | 100 |
| 1925 June | 100 | 100·7 |
| December | 100½ | 100·5 |
| 1926 June | 100½ | 100·5 |
| December | 101 | 100·9 |
| 1927 June | 100½ | 99·5 |
| December | 100½ | 99·0 |
| 1928 June | 100 | 98·2 |
| December | 99½ | 98·1 |
| 1929 June | 99½ | 97·9 |
| December | 99 | 97·8 |
| 1930 June | 98¼ | 97·4 |
| December | 98¼ | 97·1 |
| 1931 June | 97 | 96·0 |
| December | 96½ | 94·9 |
| 1932 June | 95½ | 94·1 |
| December | 94½ | 93·7 |
| 1933 June | 94 | 93·2 |
| December | 94 | 93·3 |
| 1934 June | 94 | 93·4 |
| December | 94¼ | 93·7 |
| 1935 June | 94¾ | 93·9 |
| December | 95¾ | — |
| 1936 June | 97½ | — |
| December | 98 | — |
| 1937 June | 100 | — |
| Adjusted for increase of earnings relative to rates | | |
| 1934 Year | 96 | — |
| 1935 Year | 98 | — |
| 1936 Year | 100 | — |

is that average earnings of the employed working class have approximately doubled between 1914 and 1937, while working hours have decreased more than 10 per cent. In the same period retail prices have risen about 50 per cent.

The averages conceal considerable variation in detail, and in fact a generalisation about the stationariness of wage-rates can only be justified on a general average or by reference to selected industries. Table VI shows the changes of rates in those industries which are included in the Economic Service index. The only completely unchanged rates in the thirteen years are those of Printers' compositors (time-rates) and the Trade Boards' minima for Confectionery and Tobacco; the other Trade Boards' minima, for Tailoring, Shirt-making and Boots, have moved.

Builders' wages have been related to the changes in the cost of living index. Engineers' time-rates had been relatively low in 1924, and in face of the considerable amount of unemployment in engineering industries two moderate increases have been obtained with difficulty.

The last column is filled in for reference. The entries do not in general allow for the increase in earnings apart from rates, which is discussed on pp. 107–110. When allowance is made for this and for the change in relative numbers the average for 1924 as compared with 100 in 1914 is computed to be 194 (p. 18).

After a long period of stationary time-rates shipbuilders accepted a reduction in the hope of thereby diminishing unemployment. Railway rates were reduced in 1928 and again in 1931 in consequence of the bad financial results of railway operation. The reduction was restored in 1933 and 1937. But in fact wage-rates in 1924 were relatively high (see p. 23 below).

The wages paid by Local Authorities have been influenced by those of builders' labourers. Wages for tram and lorry drivers have changed in an irregular fashion in different towns.

Agricultural wages are determined by official county minima; they were relatively low in 1924, and have remained low, in spite of the increase that took place in 1925, and of the considerable rise during and after the war.

The remaining rates included in the table are dealt with in the following section. The brief summary now given does not do justice to the continued fight against reductions and the strikes, discussions and rearrangements that have been frequent during the period. Since retail prices were falling from 1924 till 1931, the main efforts in those years were directed towards keeping rates stationary. In Mr Ramsbottom's account of 65 industries (*Statistical Journal*, 1935, pp. 665–6), 24 show a reduction of wage-rates between 1924 and 1930, 17 no change, and 24 a rise.

TABLE VI

*Changes in Wage-rates. Economic Service Index*

| | 1924 Dec. | 1928 Dec. | 1931 Dec. | 1933 Dec. | 1936 Dec. | 1937 June | 1914 as 100 Level in Dec. 1936 |
|---|---|---|---|---|---|---|---|
| Builders | | | | | | | |
|   Bricklayers | 100 | 98·1 | 94·1 | 88·1 | 93·6 | 95·8 | 161 |
|   Labourers | 100 | 97·4 | 92·9 | 88·0 | 92·8 | 95·1 | 177 |
| Engineers | | | | | | | |
|   Fitters | 100 | 103·5 | 103·5 | 103·5 | 108·8 | 110·6 | 158 |
|   Labourers | 100 | 105·0 | 105·0 | 105·0 | 112·4 | 114·8 | 199 |
| Shipbuilders | 100 | 100 | 97·0 | 92·0 | 96·0 | 100 | — |
| Compositors | 100 | 100 | 100 | 100 | 100 | 100 | 213 |
| Railways | 100 | 100 | 93·7 | 94·8 | 95·0 | 95·0 | 193 |
| Docks | 100 | 100 | 100 | 96·6 | 100 | 100 | 200 |
| Trams | 100 | 98·8 | 100·7 | 97·5 | 105·1 | 105·1 | — |
| Lorries | 100 | 98·2 | 96·2 | 95·0 | 97·5 | 97·2 | — |
| Coal-mining | 100 | 87·2 | 86·0 | 85·7 | 93·7 | (97)* | 154 |
| Cotton | 100 | 100 | 93·5 | 85·5 | 85·5 | (89)* | 155 |
| Wool | 100 | 100 | 89·5 | 80·1 | 80·1 | (87)* | 145 |
| Tailoring | 100 | 107·7 | 107·7 | 107·7 | 107·7 | 107·7 | — |
| Shirtmaking | 100 | 107·7 | 107·7 | 107·7 | 107·7 | 107·7 | — |
| Boots | 100 | 94·4 | 94·4 | 91·7 | 100 | 100 | — |
| Confectionery | 100 | 100 | 100 | 100 | 100 | 100 | — |
| Tobacco | 100 | 100 | 100 | 100 | 100 | 100 | — |
| Local Authorities' non-trading services | 100 | 98·9 | 97·0 | 94·5 | 97·4 | 99·2 | — |
| Agriculture | 100 | 112·2 | 112·6 | 111·4 | 114·6 | 117·7 | 192 |
| Weighted average | 100 | 99·4 | 97·0 | 94·3 | 97·8 | 100 | — |

* In these cases the effects of the changes in 1936–7 are a little uncertain.

## SELECTED INDUSTRIES

### Coal

Statistics are issued quarterly of the average earnings per shift of all workmen in or about mines who receive wages. It will be seen that a high maximum was reached at the beginning of 1921. After a strike and a Royal Commission, work was resumed at a great reduction, which, however, left earnings at nearly twice the pre-war level. After some further reduction in 1922 and an increase in 1923 earnings were nearly stationary till the great dispute of 1926. Early in 1927 earnings kept up, since the demand was acute after the stoppage, but then settled at about 9s. 2d. till the end of 1935. The pressure for improvement early in 1936 led to an average increase of about 7 per cent.

The average number of shifts per week has varied, but not greatly. Unemployment has been severe, but is not taken into account in these averages. Besides the wages there are some allowances in kind, the variation in which does not affect the general view.

*Earnings per man-shift worked in Coal-mines (shillings per shift).*
*Great Britain*

1914 June, 6·5 shillings

| Quarters | 1920 | 1921 | 1922 | 1923 | 1924 | 1925 | 1926 | 1927 | 1928 |
|---|---|---|---|---|---|---|---|---|---|
| First | 15·1 | 19·2 | 11·0 | 9·6 | 10·2 | 10·6 | 10·4 | 10·6 | 9·4 |
| Second | 16·9 | — | 10·2 | 9·8 | 10·9 | 10·6 | — | 10·2 | 9·3 |
| Third | 16·9 | — | 9·4 | 10·6 | 10·8 | 10·4 | — | 9·8 | 9·3 |
| Fourth | 18·5 | 12·7 | 9·4 | 10·3 | 10·6 | 10·4 | — | 9·6 | 9·2 |

| Quarters | 1929 | 1930 | 1931 | 1932 | 1933 | 1934 | 1935 | 1936 | 1937 |
|---|---|---|---|---|---|---|---|---|---|
| First | 9·2 | 9·3 | 9·2 | 9·2 | 9·1 | 9·1 | 9·2 | 10·0 | 10·3 |
| Second | 9·2 | 9·3 | 9·2 | 9·2 | 9·2 | 9·2 | 9·2 | 10·0 | 10·8 |
| Third | 9·2 | 9·3 | 9·2 | 9·2 | 9·2 | 9·2 | 9·3 | 10·0 | — |
| Fourth | 9·2 | 9·3 | 9·2 | 9·2 | 9·0 | 9·2 | 9·3 | 10·1 | — |

The movement has thus been, July 1914 to average of 1924 increase of 63 per cent., from 1924 to 1936 decrease of 6 per cent., from 1914 to 1936 an increase of 54 per cent.

## Railways

An annual report is issued by the Ministry of Transport which states the rates of wages and the average earnings of the various classes of railway workers in Great Britain in one week in the spring. Owing to the prevalence of over-time and Sunday work the earnings are considerably higher than the wage-rates. The principal change took place after a strike in 1919, when it was arranged that wages should move with the cost of living index, with the proviso that they should not fall below twice the pre-war rates. The general average before the war is stated as 27·9s. weekly in 1913. It is not clear whether this includes employees in railway workshops or not; probably their exclusion would not have much effect on the average. From 1924 the 'conciliation grades', which are in effect the operatives, other than clerks, engaged in connection with transport, are clearly separated from others.

*Average payments to the staff entered at wage-rates (shillings per week). One week in March or April*

| 1924 | 65·1 | 1929 | 66·4 | 1933 | 62·2 |
|------|------|------|------|------|------|
| 1925 | 67·3 | 1930 | 65·4 | 1934 | 62·2 |
| 1926 | 67·2 | 1931 | 65·8 | 1935 | 63·1 |
| 1927 | 67·2 | 1932 | 61·7 | 1936 | 64·4 |
| 1928 | 66·2 |      |      | 1937 | 66·1 |

The rise from 1913 is thus about 137 per cent. to 1937, while in 1924 the average was 1½ per cent. lower.

### Cotton

The *Ministry of Labour Gazette* has from 1904 shown for several industries the number of workers employed and their aggregate earnings in one week in each month, as reported by a number of firms. The returns do not always come from the same firms, and from time to time the proportion of the whole industry included has varied; but when the statistics are studied carefully, it is possible to get a fair approximation to the course of average earnings.

The corresponding average in 1914 was approximately 20s.

Apart from temporary fluctuations the movement is very close to that shown by the index-numbers on p. 21 above. An increase, however, is seen in the recent averages, which took place before 1937 without any change of rates owing to improved trade.

*Average earnings in certain firms in the Cotton Industry*
*(shillings per week)*

| Quarters | 1924 | 1925 | 1926 | 1927 | 1928 | 1929 | 1930 |
|---|---|---|---|---|---|---|---|
| First | 34·6 | 37·1 | 36·6 | 36·8 | 36·8 | 36·5 | 32·6 |
| Second | 34·9 | 37·4 | 34·7 | 37·3 | 36·8 | 36·8 | 31·4 |
| Third | 35·7 | 36·3 | 33·4 | 37·0 | 35·8 | 36·3 | 29·8 |
| Fourth | 36·9 | 36·9 | 34·2 | 36·1 | 36·8 | 34·8 | 31·3 |

| Quarters | 1931 | 1932 | 1933 | 1934 | 1935 | 1936 | 1937 |
|---|---|---|---|---|---|---|---|
| First | 30·9 | 33·5 | 31·0 | 31·8 | 31·5 | 32·4 | 35·0 |
| Second | 32·3 | 33·0 | 31·1 | 31·7 | 31·7 | 32·9 | 36·3 |
| Third | 31·7 | 31·8 | 31·5 | 31·5 | 31·9 | 33·4 | 36·5 |
| Fourth | 33·7 | 32·1 | 31·8 | 31·8 | 32·6 | 33·7 | — |

## Wool and Worsted Industries

On the same basis the figures for these industries are as follows:

*Average earnings in certain firms in the Wool and Worsted*
*Industries (shillings per week)* [1]

| Quarters | 1924 | 1925 | 1926 | 1927 | 1928 | 1929 | 1930 |
|---|---|---|---|---|---|---|---|
| First | 38·3 | 37·7 | 38·9 | 39·4 | 40·8 | 39·3 | 38·2 |
| Second | 40·0 | 36·9 | 38·0 | 40·4 | 40·2 | 40·7 | 37·4 |
| Third | 38·9 | 36·8 | 37·4 | 40·5 | 38·3 | 39·3 | 36·5 |
| Fourth | 38·8 | 38·9 | 38·8 | 40·6 | 39·7 | 40·0 | 36·8 |

| Quarters | 1931 | 1932 | 1933 | 1934 | 1935 | 1936 | 1937 |
|---|---|---|---|---|---|---|---|
| First | 35·2 | 36·1 | 34·3 | 36·5 | 35·5 | 37·2 | 39·2 |
| Second | 36·0 | 34·1 | 36·1 | 35·1 | 35·9 | 37·0 | 40·0 |
| Third | 32·9 | 33·7 | 36·7 | 34·1 | 36·6 | 37·1 | 39·2 |
| Fourth | 37·2 | 35·3 | 37·6 | 36·8 | 38·4 | 38·5 | — |

It is not possible to give an average in 1914 that certainly corresponds to those in the table, so much depends in this heterogeneous group of industries on which classes of firms are included; but a reasonable approximation is 19s., if we take the results of Mr Wood's study in the *Statistical Journal*, 1927, p. 319. But the index-numbers reached before this publication suggest a higher pre-war average, namely about 20s.

[1] The entries in the table for 1924, 5, 6 are taken from Mr Wood's paper. The *Gazette* returns before 1926 were based on too few entries to give a reliable average.

While there was no change in rates between 1924 and July 1930, earnings tended to rise till 1927. Reductions in rates took place on seven occasions from June 1930 to January 1933, amounting in all to 20 per cent. But earnings did not fall in the same proportion, and in 1936 were very little below those immediately before the first of these reductions.

In these industries the amount of employment, whether over-time or broken time is worked, varies considerably with the state of trade. Complete unemployment of individuals is partly avoided by spreading the work.

### NOTE ON THE REDUCTION OF HOURS OF WORK

A general view of the dates and amounts of reduction of hours can be obtained most readily by the consideration of four selected industries or industrial groups.

*Textiles.* In 1847 the 10-hour day Act was passed. In 1874 weekly hours were reduced from 60 to 56½, equivalent to the introduction of a Saturday half-holiday. In 1902 the last hour of Saturday's work was cut off ('so that the men could attend football matches'), and the hours were 55½. The final reduction took place in 1919, to 48.

*Building.* Summer hours in London. In 1861, 56½; 1873, 52½; 1893, 50; 1920, 44.

*Engineering.* In 1871 the 9-hour day, or rather the 54-hour week, generally replaced a former 60 hours' week, and there was little change for more than forty years, for the hours in most districts were 53 or 54 in 1914, and were reduced to 47 in 1919. In 1935 about 4 per cent. of the operatives in general engineering worked less than 47 hours in a normal week (*Ministry of Labour Gazette*, 1937, p. 135).

*Coal-mining.* In 1890 a shift of 9 or 9½ hours was usual. In 1909 there was a general reduction of 1 hour per shift. In 1919 another hour was taken off, but after the 1926 general stoppage hours were again increased, and an 8-hour shift is now general.

Giffen (*Essays in Finance*, Second Series, p. 375, ref. 75) speaks of a general reduction of nearly 20 per cent. between

1836 and 1886, 'at least in the textile, engineering, and house-building trades'. That is, from six days of 11 or 11½ hours to five and a half days of 10 hours. After the introduction of the Saturday half-holiday there was very little change till the almost universal reduction in 1919 or 1920, when the pre-breakfast period was cancelled, and from 44 to 48 hours became general, made up by nine periods, two on each of the first five days of the week and one on Saturday. An 8-hour day would be interpreted as a 44-hour week.

In the *Ministry of Labour Gazette* for the earlier months of 1937 copious information will be found in the Articles headed 'Average Earnings and Hours of Labour in October, 1935' as to the relative numbers of workpeople whose normal hours were less than 44, exactly 44, and so on to over 48.

Throughout the years there has been variation from industry to industry and place to place. The textile hours did not apply to non-textile factories or to workshops. Where work continues throughout the twenty-four hours 12-hour shifts were usual till a comparatively late date. So far as I know there has not been any elaborate study of the variation of hours or the dates of reduction in different industries, and their history may be commended to any student looking for a thesis subject.

# Chapter II

## REAL WAGES

It is evident that an account of wage changes cannot be complete till we have made allowance for changes in the purchasing power of money in the hands of wage-earners. There can be no doubt that when prices are falling and wages are constant, as was approximately the case in the periods 1892 to 1895 and 1925 to 1929, real wages are rising. Also it would be reasonable to say that when prices rose at the same rate as wages, real wages were unchanged; but even this is not certain over a period when intermediate movements had not been parallel. For example, the statistics suggest that average wages and prices each rose 20 per cent. between 1896 and 1914, but within those eighteen years sometimes prices were rising faster and sometimes more slowly than wages, and this may have induced a change in habits of expenditure; but in a short period such changes are probably numerically unimportant. In the more common periods when both prices and wages are changing but at unequal rates, to find the direction of change in real wages necessitates actual measurement of price changes. This measurement teems with difficulties both in theory and in ascertainment of the necessary data.

Clearly we must use some weighted average (weighted unless it is shown that weights are unnecessary) of price changes of the commodities purchased by the wage-earners. The familiar, and indeed the only practicable method, is to obtain an average budget of expenditure and evaluate its cost year by year. It is sometimes possible to obtain separate budgets for different classes, for example, rural and urban. It is also theoretically necessary to have budgets in different years, or at least at the beginning and the end of the period under study. But in fact we have no general collection of budgets earlier than 1904, and only one subsequent to that date, viz. in 1918, a year disturbed by the circumstances of the war.

The only measurement that we can make for the whole of the fifty-seven years we are considering is therefore the change in the cost of a budget of goods that appeared to be a reasonable standard in the year 1904. We reach such a resulting statement as that the purchase of the food, fuel, house-room, clothing, etc. which cost, say, 25*s*. in 1904, would have cost 28*s*. in 1880, 27*s*. in 1914, and 40*s*. in 1937. With the lower wages of 1880 the average budget would no doubt be modified, not by an equal proportionate reduction on every item, but by a change, for example, towards more bread and less meat. By 1937 money wages are more than double those of 1904, the diet has been modified, especially by increased variety, and considerable sums are spent on objects not included in the budget. Even the un-skilled labourer, if his real wages now equalled those of the skilled in 1880, would not be spending his money in the same way. It follows that the result of the numerical calculation of real wages by dividing the index of money wages by that of the cost of living so calculated is at best a very imperfect guide to the actual movement of real wages under any valid definition. It may be that we can assign limits of error to the calculation, so as to say that average real wages have increased something between 10 and 15 per cent. in a period, but when either wages or prices have moved considerably the possible error may be impracticably great. If this is the case, we must give up the measuring of the change and find some other way of describing it. Before discussing such methods the formation of the cost of living index series may first be explained and the result given.

The existing cost of living index is the weighted average of five series relating respectively to food, rent, clothing, fuel and miscellaneous items. The food average is itself weighted. The weights are based on the budgets of 1904, slightly modified in 1914. The index dates back only to 1914. Prior to 1914 there are series relating to food prices in London, other estimates for provincial towns comparing 1905 with 1912, and rather rough estimates for the changes in prices of fuel, of clothing and of rent for the years 1880 to 1900. The details and the method in which they are combined into a general index-number are discussed below, pp. 118 *seq*. Prior to 1880 we have to depend on the relation between retail and wholesale price changes, which is analysed on p. 122. The precision of the results is broadly ascertainable by comparing the series obtained by different methods.

An important question arises in the treatment of rent. Rates are usually combined with rents, not only in budgets but also in working-class payment, and in some periods rates have increased faster than have rents. Rates are in part the payment for the amenities of town life, in part payment for education and other services, in part of the nature of taxation. So far as the increase of rates corresponds to better services to the payer it ought not to be included in the cost of an unchanged standard of living, as intended to be measured by the index. The question is similar to that involved when a workman moves from a small provincial town where rents and rates combined are, say, 8s., to a smaller tenement in London where the combined payment is 12s. Some persons would regard the additional 4s. as worth while, since they value the company and resources of London more than provincial life. If so, there would be no rise in the cost of living owing to the transference. On the other hand, some persons regard rent and rates simply as deductive from their income, and to preserve equality wages would have to be raised by any addition to rent and rates. It is seen that there can be no certain way of measuring the effect of rates in the changing cost of an unchanged standard. In forming the index half of rates has been counted with rent, the other half is assumed to be paid for increased services and amenities. The effect of this method, which is hardly considerable, is shown on p. 119.

The resulting series of the index numbers of the cost of living is given in column 2 of Table VII. In column 1 the indices of average money wages are repeated and combined.

Column 3 is obtained by dividing column 2 by column 3 and multiplying by 100. It is not headed Real Wages, because of the numerous qualifications with which it must be used.

It is argued on p. 120 that within the definition the roughness of the data and the possible variations of treatment should lead

TABLE VII

*Index-numbers of Money Wages and of the Cost of Living,*
1880 *to* 1936

Index-numbers (1914 = 100)

| Year | Index-numbers | | | Year | Index-numbers | | |
|---|---|---|---|---|---|---|---|
| | Wages | Cost of living | Quo-tient | | Wages | Cost of living | Quo-tient |
| 1880 | 72 | 105 | 69 | 1906 | 91 | 93 | 98 |
| 1881 | 72 | 103 | 71 | 1907 | 96 | 95 | 101 |
| 1882 | 75 | 102 | 73 | 1908 | 94 | 93 | 101 |
| 1883 | 75 | 102 | 73 | 1909 | 94 | 94 | 100 |
| 1884 | 75 | 97 | 77 | | | | |
| 1885 | 73 | 91 | 81 | 1910 | 94 | 96 | 98 |
| 1886 | 72 | 89 | 81 | 1911 | 95 | 97 | 97 |
| 1887 | 73 | 88 | 84 | 1912 | 98 | 100 | 97 |
| 1888 | 75 | 88 | 86 | 1913 | 99 | 102 | 97 |
| 1889 | 80 | 89 | 90 | 1914 | 100 | 100 | 100 |
| | | | | | | | |
| 1890 | 83 | 89 | 93 | 1924 | 194 | 175 | 111 |
| 1891 | 83 | 89 | 92 | 1925 | 196 | 175 | 112 |
| 1892 | 83 | 90 | 92 | 1926 | 195 | 172 | 113 |
| 1893 | 83 | 89 | 94 | 1927 | 196 | 167 | 117 |
| 1894 | 83 | 85 | 98 | 1928 | 194 | 166 | 117 |
| 1895 | 83 | 83 | 100 | 1929 | 193 | 164 | 118 |
| 1896 | 83 | 83 | 100 | 1930 | 191 | 157 | 122 |
| 1897 | 84 | 85 | 98 | | | | |
| 1898 | 87 | 88 | 99 | 1931 | 189 | 147 | 129 |
| 1899 | 89 | 86 | 104 | 1932 | 185 | 143 | 129 |
| | | | | 1933 | 183 | 140 | 131 |
| 1900 | 94 | 91 | 103 | 1934 | 183 | 141 | 130 |
| 1901 | 93 | 90 | 102 | | (186) | | (132) |
| 1902 | 91 | 90 | 101 | 1935 | 185 | 143 | 130 |
| 1903 | 91 | 91 | 99 | | (191) | | (132) |
| 1904 | 89 | 92 | 97 | 1936 | 190 | 147 | 129 |
| 1905 | 89 | 92 | 97 | | (197) | | (134) |

For the figures in brackets in 1934–6, which are adjusted for increased earnings, see p. 18 above.

us to put ±5 against one of the terms of a comparison over such a period as 1880 to 1914, and a similar margin may be suggested for 1914 to 1936. I am doubtful whether any intelligible measurement can be made of the increase over the combined periods 1880 to 1936. If it is made, the proportion 100 to between 130 and 150 would be a reasonable margin to assign.

With similar limitations we can trace the comparative levels of prices for periods earlier than 1880. It is argued below that the relation of wholesale and retail prices in the years when they can be compared is sufficiently definite to allow an estimate of the movements of the latter from the earliest statement of Sauerbeck's index in 1846. We thus obtain the following series:

*Estimate of movement of Retail Prices*

| Average | | Average | | Average | |
|---|---|---|---|---|---|
| 1846–9 | 101 | 1880–4 | 102 | 1914 | 100 |
| 1850–4 | 101 | 1885–9 | 89 | 1924–6 | 172 |
| 1855–9 | 112 | 1890–4 | 88 | 1927–9 | 163 |
| 1860–4 | 114 | 1895–9 | 85 | 1930–2 | 145 |
| 1865–9 | 114 | 1900–4 | 91 | 1933–5 | 141 |
| 1870–4 | 116 | 1905–9 | 93 | 1936 | 147 |
| 1875–9 | 107 | 1910–14 | 99 | | |

All the retail price or cost of living series measure the change in cost of the average budget, which may be exhibited as follows:

| | Quantity | Cost in 1914 |
|---|---|---|
| Meat, etc. | 9 lb. | 5s. 7½d. |
| Bread and flour | 32½ lb. | 3s. 11½d. |
| Tea | 13 oz. | 1s. 3d. |
| Sugar | 6 lb. | 1s. 1d. |
| Milk | 9½ pints | 1s. 5d. |
| Butter and margarine | 2¾ lb. | 2s. 10d. |
| Cheese | 13 oz. | 6½d. |
| Eggs | 10 | 1s. 0½d. |
| Potatoes | 17 lb. | 1s. 0d. |
| Total | | 18s. 9d. |
| Rent | | 5s. 0d. |
| Clothing | | 3s. 9d. |
| Fuel and light | | 2s. 6d. |
| Miscellaneous items | | 1s. 3d. |
| Total | | 31s. 3d. |

The rent was sufficient for a three- or four-roomed house in the provinces and for two rooms in London. Clothing expense is in part determined arbitrarily as somewhat less than rent, partly on the basis of Mr Rowntree's investigations. The fuel is a little more than 1 cwt. of coal weekly. Miscellaneous items are mainly cleaning materials.

While the food represents the average quantities bought by the working-class families from whom budgets were obtained in 1904, and is above the minimum standard used, for example, by Rowntree, the allowance for rent, clothing, fuel and sundries is at the bare minimum. But it is to be remembered that this budget is only used for weighting the series to make the final index. If the excluded food items change in price in the same proportion as those included, we may regard the food expenditure as about 24s. in 1914, and suppose the other items to be raised also by 27 per cent., giving a total of 40s.

The average weekly income of the urban wage-earning family was probably between 30s. and 35s. in 1914. The budget therefore accounts for the bulk of expenditure at or near the average. In a period when habits of consumption and the size of the family were changing slowly, and when wages were moving in proportion to the cost of living measured on this basis, we may apply this index to the index of money wages to obtain an estimate of the change of real wages *of the urban working class whose wages were not far from the general average; that is, to the more regularly employed of unskilled labourers and to moderately skilled labourers, on the assumption that habits of expenditure had not changed.* Such a period is from about 1896 to 1914. With slight variations average real wages were nearly stationary during these twenty years. Any improvements that took place were due to imponderables, such as development of social services, and the greater variety of food and other commodities that were purchasable by those who had money unallotted to necessaries. Contrary to the general opinion, statistics indicate that the higher incomes fared little or no better in this period (see pp. 94–5).

It is possible to test the applicability of the computed cost of living index over the earlier period 1880 to 1894. There is no doubt that money wages rose and prices fell in this period. With the smaller real and money income the budget at that date would be modified in the direction of greater relative expenditure on bare necessities. If we take as a working assumption that meat, bacon, tea and sugar had only half the relative weight in the food budget that they had in 1904 as compared with bread, flour, potatoes and butter, and at the same time assume that food formed 75 per cent. of expenditure instead of the 60 per cent. above, it is found that the cost of such a modified budget fell 21 per cent. in the twenty-six years. This is to the nearest unit the same fall as is found by the 1904 budget (105 : 83, Table VII). It is generally agreed that the increase in cost of living when the standard is changing is between the limits obtained by computing the changes on the basis of the initial and final budgets (see pp. 124–6 and the references there given). We may therefore take it that the cost of living index may be used back to 1880 for the same purposes and with a similar liability to error as when it is used from 1896 to 1914. On this hypothesis average real wages rose about 35 per cent. in the decade 1880 to 1890 and a further 7 per cent. to 1896; in all 45 per cent., or with more security we may say over 40 per cent. This is the result of the combination of 15 per cent. rise in money wages and about 20 per cent. fall in prices. (Mr G. H. Wood estimates an increase of only about 10 per cent. in money wages and a fall of about 16 per cent. in prices in this period; his estimates are discussed on p. 123 below.)

When we endeavour to go back farther than 1880, all the difficulties increase. The wage data are insufficient for accurate measurement, we have to depend on wholesale prices for the change in the cost of living, and we have no budgetary information, and no guarantee that habits of expenditure have not changed in a way to vitiate the estimate to some extent. There is no doubt, however, that the directions of the movements

year by year are as given by the index-numbers of prices and
also of wages. The figure of most doubtful applicability is that
for the year of maximum prices, 1873.

The numerical results for selected dates are as follows:

### TABLE VIII

*Money and Real Wages*, 1860 to 1880

Index-numbers. Base 100 in 1914

| Columns | 1 | 2 | 3 | 4 | 5 | 6 | 7 | 8 |
|---|---|---|---|---|---|---|---|---|
| Year | Money wages | | Prices | | Quotients | | | |
| | A.L.B. | G.H.W. | A.L.B. | G.H.W. | 1 ÷ 3 | 1 ÷ 4 | 2 ÷ 3 | 2 ÷ 4 |
| 1860 | 58 | 56 | 113 | 106 | 51 | 55 | 49 | 53 |
| 1866 | 66 | 65 | 114 | 109 | 58 | 60 | 57 | 59 |
| 1870 | 66 | 65 | 110 | 108 | 60 | 60 | 59 | 60 |
| 1874 | 80 | 76 | 115 | 112 | 70 | 71 | 66 | 68 |
| 1877 | 77 | 74 | 110 | 109 | 70 | 71 | 67 | 68 |
| 1880 | 72 | 72 | 105 | 105 | 69 | 69 | 69 | 69 |

Mr G. H. Wood's figures are described below. They are
computed from his paper in the *Statistical Journal*, 1909,
pp. 102–3, equating his entries for 1880 to 72 and 105 to afford
comparison over the selected period. Since, as discussed on
p. 5, his measurement shows a smaller increase after 1880
than does the one adopted above, the first entry in the last
column would be raised to 57 for comparison with 1914. In
the period 1860 to 1880 his wage-index shows a greater rise than
does that in column 1, while his price-index shows a slighter
fall than does that in column 3. Hence in 1860 the entry in
column 5, which is the result of the computations described in
the text above, is nearly equal to that in column 8. Columns 6
and 7 illustrate the result of taking his price-index and my wage-
index and vice versa. On each of the methods we find a considerable increase in real wages between 1860 and 1866, and
another from 1870 to 1874. From 1874 to 1880 prices and wages
fell in nearly the same proportion.

If we have the temerity to compare 1860 with 1914, we should assign the limits of the index for real wages in 1860 (1914 being taken as 100) at 50 and 59, the 59 being obtained from Mr Wood's full series. Thus, if the average wage of an adult male at full work was 32s. in 1914 (p. 53), the average in 1860 would be between 16s. and 19s., when the change in purchasing power is taken into account.

The measurement of the change of purchasing power on this basis is definitely not applicable to the agricultural labourer, whose budget of expenditure is different and who depended on allowances and payments in kind to a greater extent in 1860 than in 1914. Any generalisation should be limited to urban workmen whose wages were not far from the average, and for them we should write 34s. in 1880 (p. 50) and 17s. to 20s. in 1860 instead of the amounts in the previous paragraph.

We can get a more realistic view of the change in the standard of living by making hypothetical budgets of expenditure that correspond with what we know of wages and retail prices at different dates. Careful work was done in this way for an article in *Economica* by Miss Mackenzie, 1921, pp. 221–30 (ref. 78). The assignment of quantities was made partly by the statistics of consumption per head of various kinds of food. Retail prices were determined in part from the fragmentary records that could be found, partly by the assumption that at two dates at which the wholesale prices were equal then also the retail prices would be equal. Thus Sauerbeck's index of the wholesale price of beef was the same in 1907 as in 1860; at the later date the retail price was $7\frac{1}{2}d.$, and so it was assumed that the retail price was also $7\frac{1}{2}d.$ in 1860. The budgets so obtained for the expenditure of the man whose income was at the estimated median of all incomes (working class or not) in the United Kingdom are reproduced here. It is unfortunate that the greatest uncertainty about retail prices exists for the two major items, bread and meat. In particular the price assigned to bread in 1880 appears to be too low. It is also probable that the quality of meat purchasable at $8\frac{1}{2}d.$ per lb. in 1914 was better than of that purchasable at $7d.$ in 1880. In fact, from 1880 to 1914 index-numbers of prices based on these hypothetical budgets do not show the same fall as those adopted above. If the budgets were recast I should be inclined to reduce the quantities of bread and meat in 1880, and assign $6\frac{1}{2}$*d.* per quartern instead of 6*d.* in 1860.

TABLE IX

*Estimated Budget of the Median Family in* 1860, 1880 *and* 1914

'Family' = man, wife and three schoolchildren, or 3·87 'men'

| Date: Wage: | | | 1860 20*s.* 6*d.* | | 1880 26*s.* 6*d.* | | 1914 35*s.* 6*d.* | |
|---|---|---|---|---|---|---|---|---|
| | Unit | Cal. per unit | No. of Units | Cost | No. of Units | Cost | No. of Units | Cost |
| | | | | *s.* *d.* | | *s.* *d.* | | *s.* *d.* |
| Bread | 4 lb. | 5000 | $10\frac{1}{2}$ | 5 3 | 11 | 4 7 | $10\frac{1}{2}$ | 5 3 |
| Meat | 1 lb. | 1200 | 3 | 1 $7\frac{1}{2}$ | 4 | 2 4 | 10 | 7 1 |
| Bacon | 1 lb. | 2685 | 1 | $10\frac{1}{2}$ | 1 | $11\frac{1}{2}$ | $1\frac{1}{2}$ | 1 $5\frac{1}{2}$ |
| Suet, etc. | 1 lb. | 3540 | $1\frac{1}{2}$ | 9 | 1 | 6 | 1 | 7 |
| Butter | 1 lb. | 3605 | $\frac{3}{4}$ | $7\frac{1}{2}$ | 1 | 1 3 | $1\frac{1}{2}$ | 1 $9\frac{3}{4}$ |
| Margarine | 1 lb. | 3525 | — | — | — | — | $\frac{1}{2}$ | 3 |
| Cheese | 1 lb. | 2055 | $\frac{1}{4}$ | 2 | $\frac{1}{2}$ | $4\frac{1}{2}$ | $\frac{3}{4}$ | $6\frac{3}{4}$ |
| Milk, fresh | 1 pt. | 406 | 8 | 1 0 | 10 | 1 8 | 12 | 1 9 |
| Potatoes | 1 lb. | 310 | 35 | 1 9 | 28 | 1 10 | 21 | 1 3 |
| Vegetables | — | — | — | — | — | — | — | 3 |
| Rice, etc. | 1 lb. | 1630 | 1 | 2 | 2 | 4 | 3 | 6 |
| Tea | 1 oz. | 0 | 2 | 6 | 6 | 1 $0\frac{3}{4}$ | 8 | $10\frac{3}{4}$ |
| Sugar | 1 lb. | 1860 | $2\frac{1}{2}$ | 1 $0\frac{1}{2}$ | 4 | 1 2 | 5 | $11\frac{1}{4}$ |
| Total for food | — | — | — | 13 9 | — | 16 $0\frac{3}{4}$ | — | 22 7 |
| Rent | — | — | — | 3 0 | — | 3 6 | — | 5 0 |
| Fuel, etc. | — | — | — | 1 0 | — | 1 6 | — | 1 6 |
| Clothing | — | — | — | 1 6 | — | 2 0 | — | 2 6 |
| Sundries | — | — | — | 1 3 | — | 3 $5\frac{1}{4}$ | — | 3 11 |
| Total | — | — | — | 20 6 | — | 26 6 | — | 35 6 |
| Calorie value | — | — | 87,700 | — | 94,100 | — | 106,900 | — |
| Calorie value per 'man' per day | — | — | 3240 | — | 3470 | — | 3900 | — |

The value of these budgets is not for exact calculations, but as indicating the kind of purchases probably made, and the standard of living attainable at the wages existing at early dates.

## POST-WAR MEASUREMENTS

The criticisms of the existing cost of living index are to a large extent due to confusion between change of cost and change of standard of life, but they are valid where they relate to the insufficiency of its basis for converting an index of money to an index of real wages. As regards the food budget alone, it is probable that there has not been enough variation either in the proportions of the commonest and most easily measured foods, or in the difference in price changes between these and vegetables, fruit and other commodities for which it is hardly practicable to obtain standards, to cause any serious discrepancy between the index as computed and an ideal index. Regarded as a sample the index includes a large proportion of ordinary foods, and it would need a systematic difference in the trend of prices of the residue to affect the result significantly. Again, the change in habit and some increase in the quantities of more expensive foods have an effect which has proved to be quite small when tested by cross-weighting of budgets of different dates (see pp. 124–6 below). In fact, if we take the available estimates of the general food consumption per head for 1914 (treated as not differing significantly from the average of 1909–13) and 1936 (assumed the same as 1934) and apply the changes so found to the quantities in the standard food budget of p. 31, the resulting food index-numbers lie between 126 and 131; that is, such a revision of the index gives in place of the increase of 29 per cent. shown by the Ministry of Labour's index when July 1936 is compared with 1914 the same mean with an error of ±2.[1]

---

[1] In the notation of p. 124 below the index-number of food prices based on the standard budget is $I_1 = 1\cdot29$ to $1\cdot31$, the higher number being obtained when an addition is made for fruit and vegetables, taking their price as having risen more than the general average. On the hypothetical budget based on the general changes in consumption $I_2 = 1\cdot26$ to $1\cdot28$, the higher number not only allowing for increased fruit and vegetables but also for an imagined increase of 5 per cent. in milk con-

There is not sufficient information about the course of expenditure on goods other than food, but only about the changes
of price for unchanged consumption. It is evident that there
has been an increasing margin, for the prices of necessaries
according to the Ministry of Labour's reckoning increased only
47 per cent. from 1914 to 1936, while average wages increased
90 per cent.; at the same time the average family has become
smaller. An attempt can be made to measure this margin. Take
the increased expenditure on food at 50 per cent., as argued in
the footnote below, and regard the official increases in other
commodities as minima for increases of expenditure. Also increase the budget for 1914 to 40s., allotting the additional
4s. 6d. to a margin. Thus

*Hypothetical Budgets*

|            | 1914 (p. 36) | | Percentage increase | 1936 | |
|------------|------|-----|------|------|-----|
|            | s.   | d.  |      | s.   | d.  |
| Food       | 22   | 7   | 50   | 33   | 10  |
| Rent       | 5    | 0   | 59   | 8    | 0   |
| Fuel, etc. | 1    | 6   | 74   | 2    | 8   |
| Clothing   | 2    | 6   | 89   | 4    | 9   |
| Sundries   | 3    | 11  | 70   | 6    | 8   |
| Margin     | 4    | 6   |      | 20   | 1   |
| Total      | 40   | 0   |      | 76   | 0   |

The heading 'Sundries' includes washing materials and some
small items. Suppose that in addition to the 40s. there was

sumption—imagined because Sir John Orr's figures in *Food, Health and
Income* (ref. 79, p. 54) show unexpectedly a decrease.
   From these figures it appears that there has been the usual small movement towards foods of which the price has increased less than the average.
   From the same data it is found that the measures of change of quantity
have increased about 15 per cent.: $J_1 = 1\cdot14$ to $1\cdot18$, and $J_2 = 1\cdot12$ to $1\cdot15$,
the variation again being according to the estimates for fruit and milk.
   Thus on the whole the statistics indicate that from 1914 to 1936 food
prices increased 30 per cent., quantity per head increased 15 per cent.,
and therefore expenditure on food increased per head about 50 per cent.

money available for compulsory insurance contributions. The 1914 income is then not far off the average town working-class family's when work is regular and moderately skilled. In such a case there is a free margin in 1936 of about £1 a week, instead of 4s. 6d. We may suppose that children, though less numerous, are better clothed and nourished, so that there is no saving there.

The budgets can only be regarded as approximate, but the fact that in *The New Survey of London Life and Labour* 70 per cent. of families had a margin of 20s. weekly above the bare minimum (see p. 67 below) when work was regular suggests that the margin estimated above is not exaggerated. No doubt the allocation of this margin varies greatly from family to family. In some cases they will have moved to new houses at higher rents. Very likely more fuel and light are used, and more variety of clothes are bought. The rest may be saved, used as a reserve for unemployment, or for re-establishing the budget after resuming work, spent on travel, tobacco, cinemas or in any other way. However used, this enlarged amount of free money is a very important and modern gain.

These figures at best apply only to the average. Above it we have those families where the head had skilled wages and who already had free money in 1914; there also are many younger men receiving adult wages, but without family ties. Below it, and down to incomes barely sufficient or insufficient for minimum subsistence, there are the worse-paid workmen and those with unusually great family responsibilities. The existence of all these groups is abundantly evident to any observer.

In this discussion no account has been taken of the generally reduced hours of work; the increased margin finds its use in the expenses of leisure. Nor has there been any reference to the increase of social services, which tend to mitigate the hardships of those who do not enjoy any margin.

It does not seem practicable to give any definite measurement of the change of the average standard of living in the circumstances of recent years.

# Chapter III

## AVERAGE EARNINGS AND THEIR DISTRIBUTION

### The Distribution of Earnings

In the previous chapters we have traced the change of average and of real wages paid for a full normal week, with little reference to the actual amount or the variation between classes of earners or individuals. This order of treatment was adopted because over a period more accuracy can be obtained by comparative series than by absolute estimates. A further reason for separating the study of change from that of actual amounts is that the series relating to change are based essentially on the earnings of all operatives, while for actual amounts it is absurd to average together the wages of men, women, boys and girls. Not only the rates of wages and the kinds of occupations are different between these classes, but the age distribution of males differs radically from that of females. For this purpose it is not easy to separate wage-earners from other occupied persons. The age distribution of all occupied persons in Great Britain was

|  | 1911 | | 1931 | |
|---|---|---|---|---|
|  | Males | Females | Males | Females |
| Under 16 | 52 | 77 | 30 | 57 |
| 16 to 18 | 54 | 98 | 47 | 96 |
| 18 to 25 | 183 | 320 | 175 | 317 |
| 25 to 35 ⎱ | 443 | 342 | ⎰227 | 217 |
| 35 to 45 ⎰ |  |  | ⎱186 | 128 |
| 45 to 65 | 228 | 137 | 289 | 160 |
| 65 and over | 40 | 26 | 46 | 25 |
| Total | 1000 | 1000 | 1000 | 1000 |
| Actual numbers (millions) | 12·9 | 5·4 | 14·8 | 6·3 |

With the raising of the school-leaving age the proportion of boys and girls to men and women has diminished progressively[1] and an average covering all ages would have a varying meaning as time elapsed; we should be in the same difficulty if we gave an average for boys or for girls alone. Nor for want of data can we draw a firm line between girls and women. It follows that the only definite figures we can use are for men, so far as possible after the age at which they get full adults' wages, when we wish to study changes in distribution.

Even for this limited purpose the dearth of information about the distribution of wages among persons, as contrasted with the dispersion of averages for occupations, industries, or sex or age classes, is very marked. There has been only one reasonably satisfactory general enquiry on the subject, that is the Wage Census of 1906, and even that excluded mining and agriculture. In the earlier Census of 1886, though it purports to show the distribution of the wages of individuals, it was often assumed that operatives doing the same kind of work were paid at the same rate, or more exactly that the variation of wages from the average in each occupation in the district observed was insignificant. The result is a blurring of the picture. It can, however, be used for general statements of distribution without serious error, if its limitations are understood. The more recent wage enquiries, those of 1924, 1928, 1931 and 1936, do not profess to give more detail than averages.

From the 1886 and the 1906 Censuses we can make the rough comparison on the next page.

Thus there was a shifting all up the scale, but the highest tenth gained most, 33 per cent., and successive sections below

---

[1] The table of change of average earnings, p. 30 above, is adapted for estimating the movement of the national wage-bill, when the factor 'all persons employed at wages' is applied; but it exaggerates the rise for adults, since the proportion of the younger has fallen. The difference is not great; for example, from 1911 to 1931 average wages over all have risen about 2 per cent. more than men's average. The proportion of women wage-earners to men has altered very little over long periods, but in the most recent years it has been affected by the increased unemployment among men relatively to women.

less, till the lower quartile advanced only 16 per cent. The general shape of the distribution, however, hardly changed; in both years the lower quartile is about four-fifths and the upper quartile about five-fourths of the median, and the lowest decile is about two-thirds and the highest decile about three-halves of the median. The mode, however, dominated by the wage of

*Industries, excluding Mining and Agriculture. United Kingdom*

Men's earnings in full normal week

| | 1886 | 1906 | Percentage increase |
|---|---|---|---|
| | *s. d.* | *s. d.* | |
| Lowest decile | 16 7 | 19 6 | 18 |
| Lower quartile | 20 0 | 23 4 | 16 |
| Median | 24 2 | 29 4 | 21 |
| Upper quartile | 29 5 | 37 2 | 26 |
| Highest decile | 34 7 | 46 0 | 33 |
| Mode | 22 8 | 23 10 | |
| Average | 24 11 | 30 6 | 22 |
| Per 1000 earners | % | % | |
| Under 20s. | 24 | 10 | |
| 20s.–25s. | 33½ | 21½ | |
| 25s.–30s. | 24¼ | 19½ | |
| 30s.–35s. | 11½ | 16¼ | |
| 35s.–40s. | 4¼ | 16½ | |
| 40s. and over | 2½ | 16 | |
| | 100 | 100 | |

the ordinary unskilled labourer, has dropped from near the average to near the lower quartile.

The numbers in the table above are not reliable within a few pence nor within say 2 per cent. Since these Censuses were on a voluntary basis, the returns were not proportional to the numbers employed in the industries as wholes, and approximate weighting systems have to be used. Also the range included was not quite the same in the two years. The table above rectifies these discrepancies as far as possible for comparative purposes; if only one year was taken there would be some variation from the relevant column.[1]

So far we have only two dates where the results are general. Before proceeding to approximate estimates for other dates we may consider some special returns for London. Booth obtained the wages of 75,000 adult males in 1893; this was not the result of a random sample, but represented a very large number of occupations, and, though limited by the accidents of accessibility of information, it is probably approximately typical of the general distribution. He regarded it as rather too favourable a sample, containing only the wages of men in regular employment (see *Life and Labour of the People*, Vol. vi, p. 67 (ref. 67)). In the new Survey in 1929 households were selected at random throughout London and part of its environment, and in every case the normal weekly wages of occupied members were asked. Where exact statements were refused, estimates were made from the wage-rates known to be normal for the occupations. In this way estimates were made for 94 per cent. of the families in which there was an adult male wage-earner; of these 76 per cent. were on time-wages, and these were tabulated to give a frequency distribution (p. 78, ref. 58). In such cases it is easier to compute with fair accuracy the median and the quartiles than the average and complete distribution. The comparison is more useful if made after allowance for the rise of prices, estimated for this purpose at 80 per cent. (ref. 58, p. 70), the same as obtained by comparing 1889 with the average of 1929 and 1930 in Chapter II, p. 30 above. [Table, p. 44.]

It is to be noticed that the relations between the deciles, quartiles and median in 1893 are the same as stated for the 1886 Census (p. 42); but they are modified except for the lower quartile in 1929, for the lowest decile is higher than the formula gives and the upper quartile and decile lower. The former is due to the greater rise in wages for unskilled work than for skilled,

---

[1] The above remarks are made in case it is found by some careful reader that I have published apparently inconsistent figures at different times.

as explained on p. 15 above. The latter may be due to the limitation to time-wages; it is quite likely that there has been a considerable development of piece-payments in London during the period in the higher wage groups.

*Weekly Time-wages, London. Adult males*

|  | 1893 | | 1929 | Per-centage increase |
|---|---|---|---|---|
|  | Original | Raised 80% |  |  |
|  | *s. d.* | *s. d.* | *s. d.* |  |
| Lowest decile | 21 4 | 38 6 | 43 6 | 13 |
| Lower quartile | 25 6 | 46 0 | 53 6 | 16 |
| Median | 31 0 | 55 9 | 61 6 | 10 |
| Upper quartile | 37 6 | 67 6 | 72 0 | 7 |
| Highest decile | 44 0 | 79 0 | 82 0 | 4 |

The general increase over the thirty-six years is less than that computed for the whole country (p. 30). This may be due to a combination of causes. In 1929 a number of young men earning less than their final rates were included, and generally the sample taken by Booth was of the more established workers. The comparison must be used with great caution.

The full distribution of wages in 1929 shows remarkable continuity:

*Distribution of stated weekly Time-wages for men aged 20 to 65*

London, Survey Area, 1929

| | Per 100 men | | Per 100 men |
|---|---|---|---|
| Under 34s. | 4 | 67s. 6d. to 72s. 6d. | 11 |
| 34s. to 37s. 6d. | 1 | 72s. 6d. to 77s. 6d. | 7 |
| 37s. 6d. to 42s. 6d. | 4 | 77s. 6d. to 82s. 6d. | 8 |
| 42s. 6d. to 47s. 6d. | 4 | 82s. 6d. to 87s. 6d. | 3 |
| 47s. 6d. to 52s. 6d. | 9 | 87s. 6d. to 92s. 6d. | 3 |
| 52s. 6d. to 57s. 6d. | 14 | 92s. 6d. to 97s. 6d. | 1 |
| 57s. 6d. to 62s. 6d. | 18 | 97s. 6d. to 102s. 6d. | 1 |
| 62s. 6d. to 67s. 6d. | 11 | 102s. 6d. and over | 1 |

Earnings are no longer divided into two groups, as they appear to have been a hundred years ago, corresponding to skilled and unskilled work, though in particular industries two modes may be discernible. When we merge together all occupations the modes almost disappear. This is partly because even within the same occupation there is considerable variation, partly because the standard rates for occupations which are definitely skilled vary from one trade to another, and the same is true for unskilled occupations. But an even more important consideration dominates the distribution. The line between skilled and unskilled is no longer definite, as it may have been before the introduction of automatic machinery. In modern industry there are many processes which can quickly be learnt by intelligent men, the amount of training needed varies considerably, and there is no sharp line.

We can now proceed with some hesitation to make estimates of the distribution of wages in other years. The best that I know for this purpose are contained in *Economica*, Vol. I, pp. 212 *seq.*, by Miss W. A. Mackenzie (ref. 78), from which the budgets given on p. 36 above were taken.[1]

So far as money wages were concerned the figures just given for 1886 and 1906 were modified to include mining and agriculture. The formulae that the deciles were two-thirds and three-halves and the quartiles four-fifths and five-fourths of the median were applied at other dates, the median itself being estimated by the use of the general index-numbers of money wages as given on p. 6. These formulae were used principally for the year 1860, but other methods of approximation were also employed to take in all the evidence. It may perhaps be expected that the resulting figures are correct to the nearest shilling for purposes of comparison. The deciles, not computed in the original, are subject to great error.

[1] This paper was developed from a seminar at the London School of Economics, which originally was intended to explore all the data for working-class and other earnings and expenditure from the year 1860. The work was interrupted by the war after only the preliminary stages had been covered. Miss Mackenzie brought together and completed the material collected as far as possible. I was satisfied at the time that the treatment was comprehensive and valid, and cannot hope to make any useful modifications now.

*Estimated Adult Men's wages for a full normal week.*
*United Kingdom*

|  | 1860 | 1880 | 1914 |
|---|---|---|---|
|  | *s. d.* | *s. d.* | *s. d.* |
| Lowest decile | 12 0 | 16 0 | 21 0 |
| Lower quartile | 14 6 | 20 0 | 25 2 |
| Median | 18 0 | 24 3 | 31 6 |
| Upper quartile | 22 6 | 28 0 | 39 4 |
| Highest decile | 27 0 | 36 6 | 47 0 |

These estimates allow for the shifting of relative numbers as between industries.

A bold attempt was made to extend the scope of this table to include all incomes, working or middle or upper class, by using the estimates of salaries in the intermediate group below the income-tax exemption limit, the estimated number of income-tax payers and the Censuses of Population. The results are as follows:

*Estimated Income of Heads of Households in the United Kingdom*

|  | Weekly income | | |
|---|---|---|---|
|  | 1860 | 1880 | 1914 |
|  | *s. d.* | *s. d.* | *s. d.* |
| Lowest decile | 13 0 | 17 0 | 20 6 |
| Lower quartile | 15 6 | 21 4 | 26 10 |
| Median | 20 6 | 26 6 | 35 0 |
| Upper quartile | 27 6 | 32 0 | 45 3 |

The following table gives an indication of the type of man who represented the median and quartile families of the United Kingdom:

|  | 1860 | 1880 | 1914 |
|---|---|---|---|
| Lowest decile | Average agricultural labourer | Top of agricultural labourers | Bottom of unskilled |
| Lower quartile | Bottom of unskilled | Average unskilled | Top of unskilled |
| Median | Top of unskilled | Average unskilled | Top of semi-skilled |
| Upper quartile | Ordinary semi-skilled | Top of semi-skilled | Skilled |

It is to be remarked that the cost of living fell moderately in these two periods. The rough estimates of p. 34 above give the index-numbers: 1860, 113; 1880, 105; 1914, 100.

Here the term unskilled excludes agricultural labourers. The relative and actual diminution of the latter, who have been at the bottom of the wage-scale, explains the changes in the occupants of the lower marks.

The reverse process took place in the upper parts of the scale. The number of black-coated earners increased relatively, till they reached below the upper decile and towards the upper quartile.

It is unfortunately impossible to make any reliable estimate for post-war distribution. The data for London cannot be generalised, for wages are higher in London than on the average for the rest of Great Britain, and the proportion of the middle class, if we tried to include them for comparison, would be found to be different. We must be content with the indications of the greater increase in wages of the lower skilled given above.

### Average Earnings

The principal use of computing average earnings is in connection with estimates of the National Income and of the relation of earned income to total income. Except for general purposes a statement that the average for all males or all persons is so much conveys little meaning. The variation by degree of skill and between youths and adults and again between men and women causes the average to be merely an arithmetical abstraction. Similar remarks apply to the average for one industry or for a group of industries; but in such cases it is interesting to see how far the prevalence of skilled work, as in printing, or of women's employment, as in textiles, affects the averages. It will be seen in the following tables that the averages for men are nearly the same in most of the groups shown, and the uniformity is even more marked for women.

The Wage Censuses from 1886 to 1935 allow us to estimate average earnings over the region of most large-scale industries for men, and from 1906 onwards for women employed in factories. (The 1886 Census contained no satisfactory returns for women except in textiles.) We can use supplementary estimates for men in agriculture and in mines, but there is no sufficient information for domestic service or for types of small-scale industries in which women have been employed. More detail is given of the various Censuses in Appendix A below.

If we can establish the general average with sufficient accuracy at any one date, then the index-numbers given above, p. 30, enable us to estimate it for all other dates. Those index-numbers, however, use not only the Census information but also a great mass of other data, and they are intended to relate to all wage-earners, including the groups omitted in the Censuses. The averages shown below do not necessarily tally exactly in comparison with the movements shown by the index-numbers.

Shop assistants are not classed with wage-earners for the purposes of these averages.

The Census for 1886 differed in various ways from that of 1906, and though the first table that follows places the wages for groups of industries in a form for comparison, the groups, especially the residual or miscellaneous group, are not exactly comparable. Such a change as that from wood to steel ship-building is an evident illustration of the difficulty of making comparisons of this sort over a long period.

The Census of 1906 can be compared with that of 1924 with more confidence, while those for 1924, 1931 and 1935 are sufficiently on the same plan to allow accurate comparison. Comparability has been preserved throughout the numerical operations.

Each Census, except that of 1886, gives data that allow a double computation, based either on the actual earnings in a particular week, whether full-, over-, or short-time was worked, or on the computed earnings if exactly the normal week had been worked by all operatives, though the form of the alternative data varies from one Census to another. Where the information is most complete there is very little difference in the general averages arising from one method or the other. It has seemed best, after considering the nature of the information at each date, to use full-time wages for comparing 1886 with 1906, and actual earnings for comparing 1906 and subsequent years. The results of both methods are given at the foot of Table XI and in Appendix A.

No question arises at this stage of complete unemployment. Only those who received wages in the weeks of enquiry are taken into account.

It is not possible to make any separation by age in 1924. It has not seemed worth while to show the 1928 results, since the change from 1924 was very slight, and we cannot separate even the sexes completely in the 1928 account.

The first of the two following tables shows the comparison between 1886 and 1906 over the industries for which the figures are reasonably comparable. The 1886 Census does not include building in this form. The residual group includes only police, boots, bricks, chemical manure, metalliferous mines and quarries; none is in a form that allows any important comparison with 1906. Since the other industries that make up the 1906 total, as in the second table, do not tally with this miscellany, no figure is entered for the 1906 residual. Police are not included in the subsequent Censuses, at least separately; and since their inclusion in 1886 has a definite effect on the average, that average is computed both with and without them.

On the basis of these figures, supplemented by other information, the average wage or earnings of men and boys in a full normal week, including agriculture and all other wage-earning occupations, may be put, for the United Kingdom, at about 20s. in 1886 and about 26s. in 1906. There can hardly be an error of more than 1s. in either estimate.

For adult males the averages may be put at 23s. 6d. to 24s. in 1886 and at 28s. 6d. to 29s. 6d. in 1906. In 1914 the corresponding average is about 32s. and in 1924 about 60s. By 1931 there was a slight fall of about 1s., but by 1936 or 1937 the average was again nearly 60s.

My earlier estimates for 1911, 1914 and 1924 were as follows: 'There is little risk of error in the statement that the average of a week's earnings in ordinary industry in the autumn of 1911 was £1. 9s. for men (over 20), 10s. 6d. for lads and boys, and

### TABLE X

*Wage Census of 1886 compared with 1906*

| Industries | Average earnings in full week | | | |
|---|---|---|---|---|
| | 1886 | | | 1906 |
| | Men s. | Boys s. | Males s. | Males s. |
| Coal-mining | 22·9 | 10·7 | 21·2 | 31·5 |
| Metals, engineering, ships, vehicles, metal work | 26·6 | 9·6 | 23·0 | 28·1 |
| Textiles | 23·6 | 9·2* | 19·4 | 22·9 |
| Drink | 23·5 | 9·8 | 23·0 | 25·0 |
| Wood | 25·1 | 8·6 | 21·4 | 27·1 |
| Gas, water | 26·8 | 9·6 | 26·5 | 26·4 |
| Railways | — | — | 22·0 | 25·3 |
| Miscellaneous | 21·3 | 8·5 | 20·3 | — |
| All: excluding police | 24·0 | 9·5 | 21·2 | 26·7 |
| including police | 24·6 | 9·5 | 21·9 | — |
| Agriculture | — | — | 16·3 | 18·3 |
| | Women | Girls | Females | Females |
| Textiles | 12·7 | 7·3* | 11·2 | 13·4 |

\* Two half-timers counted as one person.

£1. 6s. 3d. for all males.... The employers also stated the total amount paid in wages in 1906 and the number employed in one full week in each month. The sums as obtained (by dividing this total of wages by the average of the numbers employed) show the average annual earnings on the assumption that the same persons were employed every week that the factories were open, that is between 50 and 51 weeks, allowance being made for bank and trade holidays. In any particular week a

## TABLE XI

### *Earnings in* 1906, 1924, 1931, 1935. *Industrial Groups*

| Industries* | Average earnings (shillings per week) (See Appendix C, p. 111) | | | | | | | | At work, Oct. 1935 (in thousands) p. 105 | |
|---|---|---|---|---|---|---|---|---|---|---|
| | Men and boys | | | | Women and girls | | | | Males | Females |
| | 1906 | 1924 | 1931 | 1935 | 1906 | 1924 | 1931 | 1935 | | |
| Textiles | 22·9 | 51·0 | 48·0 | 49·2 | 13·4 | 28·6 | 26·9 | 27·5 | 391 | 617 |
| Clothing | 24·2 | 54·8 | 53·6 | 54·3 | 11·2 | 26·9 | 26·9 | 27·8 | 200 | 491 |
| Food, drink, tobacco | 23·4 | 58·0 | 57·5 | 56·6 | 9·7 | 27·9 | 28·0 | 26·6 | 294 | 204 |
| Paper, printing | 27·2 | 70·7 | 71·8 | 75·4 | 9·9 | 28·0 | 28·3 | 28·1 | 244 | 148 |
| Gas, water, electricity | 26·4 | 62·0 | 62·8 | 62·5 | 13·1 | 28·6 | 26·8 | 26·6 | 172 | 8 |
| Coal-mining | 31·5 | 53·0 | 45·2 | 44·8 | — | — | — | — | 716 | 0 |
| Metal manufacture | — | 59·9 | 54·7 | 61·5 | — | 24·5 | 24·8 | 28·0 | 229 | 14 |
| Engineering | — | 51·1 | 50·4 | 55·0 | — | 26·3 | 26·8 | 28·0 | 555 | 62 |
| Railway works | — | 69·3 | 64·0 | 68·4 | — | — | — | — | 114 | 0 |
| Vehicles | — | 57·2 | 57·3 | 65·9 | — | 26·9 | 28·6 | 31·8 | 290 | 30 |
| Ships | — | 54·3 | 51·8 | 54·2 | — | — | — | — | 91 | 3 |
| Metal Industries | — | 53·3 | 52·8 | 55·5 | — | 24·6 | 24·7 | 26·0 | 395 | 191 |
| *Total Metals* | *28·1* | *56·4* | *53·8* | *58·8* | *10·7* | *25·2* | *25·6* | *26·9* | *1674* | *300* |
| Coke, cement | — | 61·8 | 65·2 | 54·9 | — | — | — | — | 44 | 2 |
| Bricks, pottery, glass | — | 55·1 | 51·7 | 52·5 | — | 23·3 | 22·4 | 23·9 | 143 | 47 |
| Chemicals | — | 59·0 | 58·8 | 60·6 | — | 25·8 | 27·7 | 26·5 | 140 | 56 |
| *Total earth products* | *25·5* | *57·7* | *56·3* | *56·3* | *10·2* | *24·6* | *25·4* | *25·3* | *327* | *105* |
| Building, contracting | — | 59·9 | 58·2 | 56·2 | — | — | — | — | 855 | 12 |
| Wood, furniture | — | 54·8 | 52·0 | 53·8 | — | 26·3 | 27·4 | 28·1 | 175 | 31 |
| *Total Building, etc.* | *27·4* | *59·0* | *57·2* | *55·9* | *12·4* | *26·3* | *27·4* | *28·1* | *1030* | *43* |
| Other mining | — | 51·0 | 51·3 | 51·7 | — | — | — | — | 81 | 1 |
| Leather | — | 54·6 | 52·7 | 53·7 | — | 25·7 | 25·4 | 25·4 | 42 | 24 |
| Transport | — | 69·5 | 66·3 | 65·1 | — | 30·8 | 24·9 | 28·3 | 886 | 28 |
| Local Government non-profit | — | 51·6 | 52·7 | 52·7 | — | 27·8 | 26·2 | 28·0 | 270 | 21 |
| Others | — | 59·2 | 58·1 | 55·4 | — | 28·5 | 26·0 | 26·5 | 165 | 102 |
| *Total miscellaneous* | *25·6* | *63·5* | *61·6* | *60·4* | *10·6* | *28·0* | *26·0* | *26·8* | *1444* | *176* |
| Total: actual earnings | 27·0 | 57·6 | 55·7 | 56·9 | 11·8 | 27·5 | 26·9 | 27·3 | 6492 | 2092 |
| full-time earnings | 26·7 | 58·9 | 57·3 | 56·6 | 11·8 | 28·4 | 28·0 | 27·2 | — | — |
| Agriculture (men) | 18·3 | 31·5 | 35·0 | 35·7 | — | — | — | — | — | — |

\* The contents of the industries can be found by comparing these abbreviated descriptions with the corresponding classification of unemployment given currently in the *Ministry of Labour Gazette*.

certain number would be absent through illness, and throughout the year there is a margin of unemployment to take into consideration, so that the average earnings of individuals are some 7 per cent. less (less than the amounts already computed).

'To connect the occupation statistics of the Population Census with the annual earnings so calculated we have to allow not only for sickness and unemployment, but also for superannuation (since retired persons are frequently included under the occupations they used to follow) and for casual workers, who are either included under general labourers or under the occupations with which they are intermittently connected. For ordinary unemployment we have the percentage figures of the Labour Department, 3·8 per cent. in 1906; for sickness we can use the experience of the Hearts of Oak Friendly Society in 1910, which shows an average of 12 days (1·68 weeks) sickness yearly for its members between the ages of 15 and 65. The allowances to be made for superannuation (in which we may include the majority of men over 65 years) and for casual work are matters of conjecture; in the general estimate here given, about 3 per cent. has been allowed in each industry for superannuation and excessive absence from illness or unemployment of persons over 65 years, and some 3 per cent. or less for the irregularity of earnings of casual workers. Then we have the following estimate for 1906:

|  | £ |
|---|---|
| Average annual wages for employment of men and boys in 50·6 weeks (i.e. the year less trade holidays) | 66·0 |
| Allowance for ordinary unemployment 3·8 %, and sickness 3·2 % | 4·6 |
| Allowance for superannuation, etc., 3 % | 2·0 |
| Allowance for casual workers, 3 % | 2·0 |
| Average annual earnings of males, counted in the Population Census as occupied in industry | 57·4 |

'The average is raised by the inclusion of coal-mines, by the greater regularity obtained in Government and some other employments, and lowered by the inclusion of agriculture; estimates have been made for each industry separately, till all wage-earners in the United Kingdom are accounted for, with the result that the average earnings of all males occupied[1] in the sense used in the Population Census were £56·1 in 1906 and £57·4 in 1911.... This estimate includes the value of payments in kind to agricultural workers.

'For women and girls, including shop assistants and domestic servants, with little deduction for superannuation, since the majority retire on marriage, an average of £32·5 is estimated for 1911.' (*The Division of the Product of Industry* (ref. 45, pp. 28 and 30).)

'The average earnings of males of all ages classed as wage-earners is estimated in 1924 at £115, the average number of weeks worked at 44 (allowing for sickness, unemployment, and holidays), and the average earnings at full work at 52s. a week. In these averages boys are included, together with some superannuated workers and some casuals not attached to any industry; if these are excluded, we find that the average man at full work in 1924 obtained about 60s. a week. The corresponding figure for 1914 is 32s. The working week has been reduced about 10 per cent. in the period, and average *hourly* earnings of men have increased from about 7½d. to 15½d.' (*The National Income*, 1924 (ref. 47, p. 30).)

[1] That is as wage-earners.

# Chapter IV

## EARNINGS AND NEEDS

So far it has not been necessary to define the working class, but when we come to the question what proportion is in an economic position above an assigned standard, we must delimitate the whole of which we are measuring a part—delimitate rather than define, for there is no logical line to draw between the working and the middle class; for example, in the preceding chapter in general shop assistants were excluded from wage-earners, while in the final quotations they were included.

The Population Census does not distinguish social classes nor relate to income; but we can in the most recent Census make a good estimate of the number of manual workers and assign limits to the estimate. We cannot ascertain with the same degree of accuracy the number of persons who receive incomes whether from property or work. This circumstance prevents any close precision in the measurement of national income, though the error in comparison over short periods is less than when an absolute measurement is attempted.

Since the manual working class is more easily defined and is more homogeneous than the middle class, and is also more open to investigation, the first step towards classifying the population according to needs is to study the working class; we can then make rough estimates of the proportion they bear to the whole population. The definition is to some extent arbitrary. In the Town Surveys with which I have been associated we classed each family according to the occupation of the father or other principal earner; we then made a list of marginal occupations and arrived at a delimitation. Those not included were subsequently taken as part of the middle class.

In the Town Surveys the procedure was by sample. The

'universe' from which the sample was taken was the houses or tenements in a defined region, and, a list having been obtained of these, one household in thirty or fifty (the number varied from one enquiry to another) was visited, and its economic condition ascertained as accurately as possible. Earlier Surveys, namely Booth's *Life and Labour of the People* in 1889 *seq.* (ref. 67) and Rowntree's *Poverty* (York) in 1899 (ref. 81), were complete as far as they went, not samples. The more recent Surveys are those of five towns, Reading, Northampton, Warrington, Stanley, and Bolton, in 1912–14 and 1924, published as *Livelihood and Poverty* and *Has Poverty Diminished?* respectively (refs. 53, 54); *The New Survey of London Life and Labour,* 1929–32 (refs. 57, 58)[1]; *The Social Survey of Merseyside,* 1929–32 (ref. 77); *Work and Wealth in a Modern Port* (Southampton), 1932 (ref. 73); and *A Survey of the Standard of Living in Sheffield,* 1933 (ref. 90); *A Social Survey of Plymouth,* 1935 (ref. 91).

Booth obtained information about every family in the County of London from which children were known to the School Attendance Officers. From this observed 'universe' he generalised with a considerable loss of precision to include other working-class families. He also took as a unit of classification a street as a whole, and compared the result with the 'universe' of families. Rowntree obtained information from every working-class family except a small margin. Neither gave an explicit definition of the working class.

In the more recent Surveys there have been three main objects: to classify the incomes of families in relation to their needs over the whole scale of working-class families; to find what proportion and what numbers were in poverty; and to make comparisons from place to place and from one year to another.

The earlier enquiries were principally directed to the second of these, and we have therefore to describe the use of the word poverty. For the third purpose, that of comparison, it is less

---

[1] Abbreviated to *New London Survey* in further references.

important to labour at a theoretical definition of poverty than to make it exact and intelligible, and to keep it absolutely unchanged in comparisons. Any minimum is arbitrary and relative. Even if it were the case that the estimates of the calorie content of food as digested were precise, and if it were known what *quantities* of vitamins were present in milk, fruit, etc. and how much was required for healthy persons of different ages, it would still be true that different degrees of health and efficiency would call for different quantities. At the one extreme it is the diet that would just support an inactive life without impairment of vitality, at the other the greatest expenditure that could be applied without waste to keep a man at maximum efficiency in the most exacting work. In feeding oxen there is a point where an increase of expenditure will no longer be met by an increase in the value of the resulting meat, and no doubt practical farmers are aware of the balance; but experiments on human beings are not so easy and the objective can only be defined for sheer muscular work. Such experiments as have been made are inconclusive. It is well known that the English labourer has existed and brought up families on diets that would be regarded as semi-starvation now, and that some continental workmen and most Eastern have had, and in some cases still have, an apparently even more penurious diet.

We are not considering now an optimum diet, nor one that in present conditions should be taken as the official administrative minimum; when the wealth of a country increases that can be raised. But we must have some definite scale below which a family can certainly be said to be in want. For comparisons with the past we must take the scale of the earlier writers. For the future it would be reasonable to raise the scale.

Booth's class of 'very poor' was described by him as ill-nourished and ill-clad; his 'poor' class is neither ill-nourished nor ill-clad 'according to any standard that can reasonably be used' (Vol. I, p. 131), its members are not 'in want', though they would be much the better off for more of everything. These two classes are taken as below the line of poverty, which he defines no more accurately than this, at least in words. But this leads to a definite statement of income, viz. about 23s. weekly for a moderate-sized family in 1890 in London, and this sum can be translated with the help of the budgets of expenditure he gives in terms of food, clothing, rent, etc. Close examination of these data showed that the food gave just the minimum amount of calories that were computed by physiologists to be necessary and used to establish a minimum line by Rowntree and subsequent investigators. It is difficult to understand with modern ideas how those with less than this minimum could be described as 'neither ill-nourished nor ill-clad'.

With such difficulties in assigning food minima, it is not surprising that the standard for other classes of expenditure is purely conventional. As regards clothing, if we assume that hats, boots and socks are necessaries, and recognise that pro-tection against cold and wet is essential, we can make a rough estimate, based on actual habits and expenditure, of the cost of clothes as purchased by the poorer sections of the working class. Nothing is allowed for ornament. Booth gave no de-finite figure, but took under 2s. weekly for a moderate family; Rowntree put it at 2s. 3d. for parents and three children. The corresponding figure in the *New London Survey* was 5s., which allowed for the rise in prices.

Fuel is more definite, since the fire necessary for cooking and washing may also be sufficient for heating. Light is so small an item in a poor household that an arbitrary sum may be added for it. For soap and other household necessaries also a small sum can be assigned.

There remains the difficult question of rent. In the *New London Survey* Booth's and Rowntree's method was followed by taking the rent actually paid as the minimum. Booth found it to be rather more than one-fifth of the total expenditure, while Rowntree took a slightly smaller proportion. In the *New London Survey* the proportion was about the same. In each case this is at the poverty line; the proportion falls, but not rapidly, as income increases. In London a supplementary study was made to find how far rent was a cause of poverty on the one hand, and whether families in poverty were actually short of house-room on the other.

While Booth's classification was based on the impression given by all the circumstances of the family as well as on its visible income, Rowntree, and the compilers of the *New London Survey* and also of the 'five towns' enquiries, subtracted from income rent as actually paid, and compared the remainder with other minimum requirements. The justification for this method lies in the fact that a man is not free to adjust his rent to his income and needs, but must get what accommodation is available with reference to his work. When this method is used, the question of the adequacy of the accommodation can be discussed separately.

The alternative method of computing the minimum size of a tenement that would accommodate each family, and its cost when it is in a satisfactory condition, is abstract, since such houses are not always available, and it also depends on what is considered necessary in housing. The standard now aimed at is far superior to that which the poor have hitherto reached, and it is doubtful whether if expenditure was completely uncontrolled by custom or law, money would not be devoted to other objects rather than to the rent of a house that satisfies modern ideas.

The minimum as defined or described by Booth or Rowntree, and followed to ensure comparability by later investigators, is more inadequate than was formerly believed for the families where there are young children. The discrepancy is partly due to incomplete arithmetic. There is a scale of requirements by age and sex based on the amount of calories needed. The cost to an adult is computed, and that for a child is assigned by applying to this cost the smaller number of calories he is supposed to need. This process assumes that the *cost* of 1000 calories is the same for the diet of a child as for that of an adult. Now milk, reckoned in calories, is an expensive form of food. In London in 1928 one penny bought 130 calories if spent on milk, but 570 if on bread, 600 on margarine, 730 on sugar. It is therefore necessary for completeness to construct adequate dietaries at minimum cost for different ages. The protein content also needs examination, but the numerical effect is smaller, since bread is the cheapest source of protein, unless we distinguish animal from vegetable protein and emphasise the former.

A great deal depends on what quantity of milk is necessary for a child's healthy growth, and whether other foods can be substituted for it. Not enough is definitely known on this subject, but there are very good reasons for giving more than is necessary so as to be on the safe side. The deficiency in the diets is not serious if they are regarded not as ideal, but in relation to customary working-class expenditure. The minimum allows 2½ pints weekly for a child, that is, a third of a pint daily. In 1933 a Committee of the British Medical Association considered the minimum cost of an adequate diet, and by increasing the allowance of milk for children and including more fruit and vegetables, so as to ensure a supply of vitamins, arrived at a higher minimum. The Ministry of Health Advisory Committee on Nutrition in 1936 advocated also a greater consumption of milk by adults. A complete discussion of the various diets proposed is to be found in 'A New Calculation of the Poverty Line', *Journal of the Royal Statistical Society*, 1937, pp. 74 *seq.*, by R. F. George (ref. 74). From this the following figures are deduced:

*Cost of minimum diets, July 1936, per week*

|  | New London Survey | | British Medical Association | | Ministry of Health | |
|---|---|---|---|---|---|---|
|  | s. | d. | s. | d. | s. | d. |
| Adult male | 6 | 0 | 6 | 5 | 6 | 9 |
| Adult female | 5 | 0 | 5 | 4 | 5 | 9 |
| Child aged 5 to 14 | 2 | 10 | 4 | 8 | 5 | 5 |
| Child under 5 years | 2 | 0 | 3 | 3 | 3 | 10 |
| Total for such family | 15 | 10 | 19 | 8 | 21 | 9 |

In 1929 prices were higher and the minimum actually used in the *New London Survey* was 7*s*. 1*d*. for an adult male and 19*s*. for such a family. The results of applying a scale for children similar to that of the British Medical Association to the *Survey* data are given below (p. 65).

Vitamins were of course not known in Booth's time, though the importance of fruit and vegetables as constituents of diet has always been realised. Since the amount of vitamins needed for normal adults is not known, nor how much is provided in an ordinary mixed diet, it is not really possible to know whether the 7*s*. taken as the minimum for a man in ordinary work in London in 1929 needs to be raised on the ground that the food purchasable for that sum was deficient in vitamin content. It does allow of a budget balanced in other respects (protein content, etc.) with the mixed meat and vegetable diet to which the town labourer is accustomed. It is not, however, a minimum if a more vegetarian diet is taken. The agricultural labourer obtains the necessary calories and protein by a larger consumption of bread, and especially of potatoes, and less meat, with enough vitamins (except where they are only to be found suitably in fresh milk, which is sometimes difficult to obtain on farms), the whole at a lower cost than in the town budget. Dr A. Hill shows this in his study of diets in Essex[1] (ref. 76).

This detail has been necessary because there has been much discussion recently on the cost of an adequate diet. There is no doubt that more than the lower minimum is usually spent and spent with advantage. If we were beginning this kind of investigation now, we should probably put the poverty line higher, as the Americans do. But there is a tendency to try to state as a minimum that which is desirable, or even is an optimum diet, in a modern industrialised country, and this eludes definition even more than does a physiological minimum. The measure-

[1] A daily ration, not to be recommended, consisting of 2 lb. of bread, ¼ lb. of cheese and ¼ lb. of sugar, together with garden produce, yields the necessary calories, protein and probably vitamins for an adult male. This would cost in 1936 about 4*s*. weekly.

ment on Booth's scale is at the same time easier to make precise and is more in accordance with the ideas of poverty and want as distinct from discomfort.

Since the poverty line is descriptive rather than logical, it is well to form some idea of the standard of living reached on it. In London in 1929 the minimum for a workman with wife and two children of young school age was put at 39s. weekly. Of this 9s. 4d. was allotted to rent, nearly a quarter of income; this would pay for two rooms with a scullery, and is on the margin of overcrowding. 2s. 4d. goes for travelling to work and for unemployment and health insurance. 4s. 2d. is allotted to clothes, 3s. for fuel (1¼ cwt. weekly), 1s. 2d. for cleansing materials, etc. There is left 19s. for food. There is no surplus for beer, tobacco, amusement, trade-union subscription or voluntary expenditure of any sort. Emergency can only be met by some windfall or by stinting food or clothes. None the less it affords a living at a higher standard than has had to suffice in earlier generations for the existence of a great part of the working class. This has been chosen as the fixed basis from which to compute, and it gives a description of the poverty line and incidentally a definition of poverty.

With the minimum so computed for each family we have to compare its income. Here again we come to difficulties of definition. The unit is the family, consisting of all persons related to each other who sleep in the same tenement. The total income is the sum of the earnings of all working members, together with income from property, if any, including the value of a house owned and occupied, and pensions arising from former employment. Old-age pensions are usually included as income.

In all post-war investigations a distinction has been made between the income that would accrue if all normally occupied members of the family were working the number of hours customary in their occupation and the income actually received in the period of investigation, that is, the former diminished by unemployment or temporary illness, and increased by over-

time. To the income thus observed was added sickness and
unemployment benefit if it was on a contributory basis. At the
date of the *New London Survey* non-contractual unemployment
payments, the dole and allowances under the means test, if they
existed at all, were not important. Till recently it was not
necessary to decide whether charity or public assistance was
to be classed as income, since the amounts so received were
rarely sufficient to bring the family above the poverty line;
they would meet food requirements, but not rent and clothing.
But in the most recent Survey, that by Dr Ford on Southampton, a more detailed analysis is given of the proportion of
income received from such sources. In general the relation to
the poverty line is tabulated twice, the first assuming full-work
income, the second on the actual income.

No definite calculation has been practicable for deducing the
average amount of poverty over a year from these tabulations.
When 'unemployment is not acute there are many families in
fair circumstances who can tide over periods of illness or unemployment or short-time out of savings or credit. When
unemployment is severe more and more families exhaust their
resources. Also a proportion of workmen never get more than
intermittent work, and the nominal full-time earnings are far
above their average earnings. In London, where unemployment was sub-acute at the time of investigation, the results of
the alternative enquiry on Booth's plan of taking a street as the
unit yield a percentage in poverty approximately the same as
that arising from the sample based on actual income. This is
probably the best single figure to take for most purposes; it
may either be regarded as a minimum, or be based on a special
definition of poverty that includes temporary poverty. But it
is to be remembered that during a year some of the families
that were above the line in the week of investigation would fall
below it in some other week, so that it is difficult to get a clear
short definition of the meaning of the percentage.

The process of comparing the aggregate of incomes of
members of the family with the family needs assumes that the

whole income is pooled if necessary. Where family ties are
strong, or where additional earnings come from the wife or
young workers, the assumption is justified; but when the income is that of elder brothers or sisters, they may not be willing
to hand over all surplus above their special needs to the support
of an unemployed parent or other children. The experience of
the opposition to the means test affords some evidence on this
point. An analysis on the subject was made in the *New London
Survey* (Vol. VI, p. 109) as follows:

A computation was made on the hypothesis that supplementary earners, other than wives and orphans, were removed
from the family; the needs are less for the remainder, but the
income in most cases is further diminished. In the week of investigation the percentage of families below the line was raised
from 9·8 to 12·2; in a full-time week the proportion is raised
less, namely from 5·7 to 7·5.

We must consider the proportion of persons in poverty as
well as the proportion of families; that is, we must take the
individual as unit, as alternative to the family as unit. The proportion is increased if an excessive number of children below
the earning age are present in the poor families, and decreased if
there are many cases of old people living alone or as couples for
whom the old-age pension does not suffice. The latter group
predominated in London, and instead of 9·8 per cent. of families,
we find 9·1 per cent. of persons in families below the poverty
line in the special week; in the full-time week the reduction is
greater, from 5·7 to 4·6 per cent.

All these percentages apply to the working class living in
families or at least in private tenements. For completeness we
should add those in workhouses and some other institutions
for the numerator and add the middle class for the denominator.
The institutional population raises the poverty percentage
for individuals by about one part in ten. In the *Survey* area,
which included nine contiguous predominantly working-class
boroughs with the County of London, it was estimated that
the proportion of working-class households to all households

was 72 to 28, and that of persons in the two classes nearly the same.

The results obtained from the various definitions may be thus tabulated:

*Percentages below the poverty line. The New Survey of London Life and Labour, 1929–30*

|  | Persons | | Families | |
|---|---|---|---|---|
|  | Working class | All | Working class | All |
| Excluding institutions | | | | |
| Full-time | | | | |
|   Incomes pooled | 4·6 | 3·3 | 5·7 | 4·1 |
|   Incomes not pooled | 7·6 | 5·5 | 7·5 | 5·4 |
| Week of investigation | | | | |
|   Incomes pooled | 9·1 | 6·6 | 9·8 | 7·0 |
|   Incomes not pooled | 13·2 | 9·5 | 12·2 | 8·8 |
| Including institutions | | | | |
| Full-time | | | | |
|   Incomes pooled | 5·0 | 3·6 | — | — |
|   Incomes not pooled | 8·4 | 6·0 | — | — |
| Week of investigation | | | | |
|   Incomes pooled | 10·0 | 7·2 | — | — |
|   Incomes not pooled | 13·4 | 9·7 | — | — |

In the Street Survey the percentage of working-class persons in poverty was estimated as 11·6 (Vol. vi, p. 126), adjusted to 8·7 for the whole population (p. 148).

We have thus twenty-six or more estimates, varying from 3·3 to 13·4 per cent., of the proportions in poverty, any one of which might be quoted legitimately, if accompanied by a definition of the scope and method. It is evident that great care is necessary in making comparisons in place or time to secure uniformity of definition.

Very little difference is made in these percentages if measurements of housing accommodation are introduced into the minimum. It is sufficient to refer the reader to the analysis in Vol. vi, p. 93 for the results.

Special reference should be made to the proportions of children in families below the poverty line. It is to be expected *a priori* that relatively more children than adults would be found in poverty, because in a group of families of unskilled workmen it is those with most dependents that fail, and because it is believed that families are larger at the lowest position on the economic scale; on the other side there are the old people living by themselves with insufficient means. In fact, on the assumption of full earnings nearly 20 per cent. of the persons over 65 years had insufficient means (though these were usually supplemented by poor relief), about 3 per cent. of those between the ages of 14 and 65 were below the line, and 6 or 7 per cent. of the children. In the week of investigation, since the main burden of unemployment is on adults with dependents, the percentage for children is raised to 13, while that for the old is 22, and for the ages 14 to 65, 6½. It may also be remarked that the proportion living in overcrowded conditions was much greater among children than among adults.

The above paragraph relates to the minimum as used for the general comparisons. In order to ascertain the position under the scale raised approximately to the British Medical Association's scale (for children only) the cards were re-examined and an extra 12*d.* to 25*d.*, according to age, was added to the children's minimum. The result was to bring the percentage for children on the full-time basis up to that in the week of investigation on the old basis, as is seen in the table on p. 66. The addition to the latter figure, which has not been computed, would be less (ref. 61).

Perhaps a more realistic meaning is given to the poverty line if we regard the minimum as the total of fixed charges on income, and examine the extent of the surplus. This surplus is available for optional purchases, some of which are in fact made by the poor at the expense of necessaries. The first choices are what are called conventional necessaries; for instance, funeral insurance, cinemas or other amusements, sweets, tobacco, beer and newspapers. Here, or indeed among necessary expenditure in many cases, should be put payments to trade unions. Then

*Working-class families. Percentages below the poverty line.*
*London Survey Area, 1929–30*[1]

|  | Full-time earnings | | | Week of investigation. Old basis |
|---|---|---|---|---|
|  | Old basis | Additions | Total |  |
| Families | 5·7 | 1·6 | 7·3 | 9·8 |
| Persons |  |  |  |  |
| Males over 14 | 2·5 | 1·4 | 3·9 | 6·5 |
| Females over 14 | 5·0 | 1·4 | 6·4 | 8·5 |
| Children: 5–14 | 7·0 | 6·5 | 13·5 | 13 |
| 3–5 | 5·5 | 6·5 | 12 | 13 |
| 0–3 | 5·5 | 5·5 | 11 | 13 |
| All | 4·6 | 2·7 | 7·3 | 9·1 |

comes a general improvement in diet, more meat and greater variety. Also clothes have been cut down to an unsatisfactory minimum, especially for young people earning their own living. Rowntree has described a standard in *The Human Needs of Labour*[2] (ref. 82), but it has not been practicable to apply it to the London data. Mr Caradog Jones, in *The Social Survey of Merseyside*, put it at 50 per cent. above the minimum for every family, and found that 30 per cent. of the Merseyside working class failed to reach it. No general statement can be given on this basis for London, without reworking from the original cards, but it may be remarked that it was found that the median wage of a workman on full-time was 62s. 8d. in 1929. This is over 50 per cent. more than the minimum when he has a wife and two children to support, but gives less than 50 per cent. surplus for three children. But the majority have less than three children on an instantaneous survey; this method is unsatisfactory, and we can proceed more definitely as follows.

Taking the family income for weeks of full employment, the average for London was found to be 78s. weekly. The average for minimum needs was about 44s., so that necessities account

---

[1] From the *Journal of the Royal Statistical Society*, 1936, p. 365.
[2] First published in 1918. Completely revised in 1937.

for about 56 per cent. of all income in a full week, increased to 60 per cent. in the week of investigation. The unallotted income is nearly £80 per annum averaged over all working-class families. This average of course conceals very wide variations, which we can analyse. Above £2 a week margin there were 36 per cent. of the families; from £1 to £2, 34 per cent. If one were asked for a general figure for an excess over the minimum which gave reasonable freedom and comfort, a practical sufficiency, one might name £1 weekly, and say that 70 per cent. of the London working-class families attained this standard when at full work. If we lower the excess to 10s., we include a further 14 per cent. A further 10 per cent. had less than 10s. margin, and may be considered as approaching poverty, or at least as having an inadequate margin for emergencies. The remaining 6 per cent. were below the line in a full week (Vol. VI, p. 110).

We cannot generalise from London to Urban England. When in 1902 Rowntree argued that the York experience gave nearly the same percentage as Booth's London twelve years earlier, he was comparing the results of different methods and lines of approach. The only post-war investigations which were deliberately made on the same basis have been London 1929–30, Merseyside 1930, Southampton 1931, Sheffield 1931, and Northampton, Warrington, Reading, Bolton and Stanley in 1923–4. For the full week's income the percentage of working-class families below the standard varied from 2 in Bolton to 9·5 in Merseyside. Since the incidence of unemployment was very different at the different dates and localities, the variations in the returns for the weeks of investigation were wider; the percentages were Southampton 20, Merseyside 17, Sheffield 15·4, Reading 11, London 10, Warrington 8, Stanley 7·5 (at a date when coal-mining was fairly active), Bolton 7·5 (before the main depression in the cotton industry) and Northampton 4. It is evidently futile to try to compute an average from these data.

Though we cannot generalise in space, it is possible to make some comparisons in time, viz. London in 1930 with London in 1890, and for certain provincial towns before and after the war.

Sir Hubert Llewellyn Smith, who had taken part in the original Life and Labour Investigation, conducted as part of the *New London Survey* enquiries on exactly the same lines as had Booth. That is, the School Attendance Officers brought their books and for each street-section gave what information they had for every family in which there were children aged from 3 to 14. The officer would not generally have any detailed knowledge of the actual family income, but he usually knew enough of the occupations of the principal earners to give a fair idea of their average earnings when in work (Vol. III, p. 112). This information, combined with data from many other sources, was used to determine the colours on the maps which gave a graphic view of the distribution of poverty and sufficiency throughout London for comparison with Booth's well-known 'poverty maps'. But here we are rather concerned with numerical measurements. Following Booth's method each family was assigned to a grade as very poor, poor, and so on up the scale. There were many statistical difficulties in passing from these records to the population as a whole, which were surmounted at both dates with reasonable precision. In both years it was assumed that the population with school children was similar to the whole working-class population. It was verified from the enquiry by sample at the later date that this was very nearly justified as regards families, but that it overestimated the number of persons in poverty, since the poor families with children were naturally larger than those without.

Keeping as closely as possible to Booth's methods, it was found that in 1929–30 in the County of London 9·6 per cent. (9·5 if the outer boroughs are included) of the population, including the middle and upper classes, were to be classed as poor; in 1889–90 the corresponding percentage was 30·7. These are the essential figures for the most definite comparison in time. The variant figures on p. 64 above are on different definitions and methods.

A useful way of making comparisons from time to time or place to place is to depend not on the proportion that have reached a certain standard but on the standard reached by a certain proportion. Thus, if we can find the economic situation of the median or quartile man or family, we can often make comparisons more precisely and with more human interest than when we use the arithmetic average. Some examples of this method are given on p. 46.

For London the only proportion we have for comparison is Booth's 30·7 mark, or rather the 37·3 per cent. he found when only the working class was in question, the middle class in his London being about one-sixth of all. Taking this as 37½ per cent., or the third 'octile' if the word may be allowed, and reckoning up from the bottom, the poverty line was reached in Booth's time, but about 24s. above it in 1930. That is rather more than is suggested above as a reasonable margin for comfort, when we take the full-time week statistics; for the special week the position is about 19s. above the line—in both cases taking the family as the unit. This extra £1 reaches the standard of living of a partly skilled workman with a wife and two dependent children, and with no income other than his wages.

For the important intermediate period 1913 to 1923 we find the following comparison in *Has Poverty Diminished?* p. 18:

*The five towns, Northampton, Warrington, Bolton, Reading and Stanley, aggregated*

Percentage in each group below standard.

| Working class only | 1912–14 | 1923–4 | |
|---|---|---|---|
| | | Full week | Special week |
| All persons | 12·6 | 3·5 | 6·5 |
| All earners | 6·9 | 1·6 | 3·6 |
| All non-earners | 17·2 | 5·2 | 8·9 |
| All men (over 18) | 7·2 | 2·0 | 4·2 |
| All women (over 16) | 9·4 | 2·7 | 5·0 |
| All boys and girls over 14 | 10·5 | 4·1 | 7·3 |
| Children (under 14) | 21·6 | 6·4 | 11·3 |

During these ten or eleven years 'while wages have risen towards meeting needs, these needs themselves have fallen towards meeting wages, with the reduction in the number of children'. 'In the aggregate of the towns the improvement due to increased wages is about twice the improvement due to diminished needs. In the special week, however, two-thirds of the improvement due to wages was lost...owing to unemployment' (pp. 22–3).

The statistics available for the subject-matter of this chapter are sporadic and incomplete, but they will serve to give some body to the rather abstract account of the movements of average wages of the previous chapter.

# Chapter V

## THE NATIONAL WAGE-BILL

The term National Wage-Bill is here used for the aggregate paid in wages in a year in a defined country. As regards the country, a difficult transition is needed at the date that South Ireland ceased to be part of the United Kingdom. Subsequently to that date the area considered is Great Britain and Northern Ireland. In pre-war statistics the whole of Ireland has been included both in the index-numbers of wages and in estimates of average wages; and in total income it is not possible to separate the incomes of persons resident in Ireland from those of persons resident in Great Britain. The only available plan has proved to be to make estimates for Great Britain and Northern Ireland in 1924 and subsequently, and to discount the 1913 estimate for the part due to South Ireland, when comparison is made between the estimates for years before and after the war. For this purpose it has been estimated that the aggregate income of South Ireland was about 5 per cent. of that of the United Kingdom, while the wages were a slightly smaller proportion.

The delimitation between wage-earners and salaried, or between manual workers and others, already alluded to (p. 54), must be worked out from the Occupation Tables of the Censuses of Population. The detail of the separation here applied is given in full in Appendix E below. In this, shop assistants have all been classed as non-manual, partly for reasons there given, partly because the wage-index does not include their wages or salaries for want of data. It seems to be impossible to get over this difficulty completely; for example, in the *New London Survey* working-class families were defined on the basis of the occupation of the head of the household, and the relevant instruction was 'Shop assistants to be ranked working class unless their work is managerial or supervisory' (Vol. III,

p. 416). On the other hand, in the 'five towns' investigations there were excluded as non-working class 'all shop assistants except butchers, fishmongers, grocers, greengrocers and bakers' (*Has Poverty Diminished?* p. 28). This instruction applies to the head of the household; but there are very many cases where the head is a manual worker and a daughter a shop assistant, so that the definition cuts across families.

The procedure first suggested, if not dictated, by the available statistics is to exclude shop assistants from the manual-working class; but in fact they were included in the 1911 and 1924 estimates. In Table XII, p. 76 below, the number of earners' index relates to estimates where shop assistants are excluded. Strictly, up to 1911 the total wages column excluding them should be used, and subsequently that including them, the two series being taken independently of each other. Actually, they are proportional, it being assumed that their earnings were an unchanged proportion of all. In fact, it is not very important to make the distinction, since the scale of payments overlaps manual wage-rates, and the aggregate is only a small proportion of total wages. In any case it is essential to make clear what has been done in this respect. In the aggregate of all incomes the decision becomes unimportant, so long as these payments are included somewhere.

The sums counted as wages are the payments before the compulsory contributions to insurance are deducted, and without addition of the employers' contributions; this is the procedure necessitated in the construction of the wage index-numbers. The numbers receiving wages are exclusive of those completely unemployed. When it comes to computing total national income, the workers' payments come back as part of unemployment benefit, and there is an addition to be made for the employers' contributions, while the place of the additions made by Government must be weighed with other transfers of income, if we are considering, not the wage-bill, but the total money receipts of the working classes.

The method here adopted is as follows. The index-numbers

of average wages estimated above are the starting-point. These are multiplied by a series, also in index-form, proportionate to the number of persons employed in working-class occupations.[1] The product is discounted by the percentages unemployed. The result is a series of index-numbers representing the change in the wage-bill. The actual amount of the wage-bill is then estimated from the Census of Wages or otherwise at any one date, and thence its amount can be computed at other dates. In practice estimates are made as independently as possible at more dates than one, and so the precision of the series is controlled. This rather involved and indirect procedure, by series rather than by direct computation, is necessitated by the data, if we are to preserve comparability.

For the computation of the basic wage-bill the Wage Census of 1906[2] was the starting point, modified to the year 1911 so as to use the Population Census of that date, and extended so as to include occupations not dealt with in the Wage Census (see pp. 51–53 above). The average weekly earnings so found were reduced so as to apply to all persons classified as occupied in manual work in the Population Census, a method which was more convenient than estimating separately the numbers of superannuated and casual workers and their earnings, though rough assessments of these were implied.

In addition, systematic allowance was made, before annual earnings were computed, for holidays, unemployment and sickness.

The results may be re-tabulated as follows, it being understood that the decimals are only working figures with spurious accuracy.

[1] The numbers occupied are based on the age limits 15 and 65. Thus the wages of children are ignored, including those of half-timers. The numbers are not the same as the insured population, since this excludes those under 16 years, excludes agriculture and domestic service, and includes a considerable number of salaried.

[2] It would have been possible to work from the Wage Census of 1924 and the Population Census of 1921, but the former was incomplete at the date the 1924 estimate (ref. 47) was made.

*Earnings in* 1911

Males

| | |
|---|---|
| Average per week :—fully employed | 26*s*. |
| discounted for old and for casual workers | 24·44*s*. (*a*) |

Number of weeks worked : 52 less

| | |
|---|---|
| holidays | 1·4 |
| sickness | 1·664 |
| unemployment | 1·976 |
| 5·04 = | 46·96 (*b*) |

| | |
|---|---|
| Numbers occupied according to Population Census | 11,000,000 (*c*) |
| Annual Earnings: product of (*a*), (*b*) and (*c*) | £631,000,000 |

Females

| | |
|---|---|
| Average per week in Industry | 11*s*. 10*d*. |
| Raised to include domestic servants and shop assistants | 13*s*. 8*d*. (circa) (*a*) |
| Number of weeks worked | 48 (circa) (*b*) |
| Number occupied according to Population Census | 4,600,000 (*c*) |
| Annual Earnings: product of (*a*), (*b*) and (*c*) | £151,000,000 |

To these totals add £20 Mn for soldiers and sailors abroad, and we reach the estimate for the total wage-bill, viz. £802 Mn.

It is evident that the unit 2 is of no significance, and that there is a margin of error, which may be of ± 5 or even 10 per cent. in the computation. For comparison with 1924, however, the margin is lower, since the computations were as nearly as possible on the same basis.

The estimate for 1924 is described in detail in *National Income in* 1924, Chapter IV (ref. 47). It is summarised as follows:

*National Wage-bill (in £ millions). United Kingdom*

| | Males | Females | Total |
|---|---|---|---|
| Computed for 1911 | 631 | 151 | 782 |
| Adjusted to 1914 | 682 | 163 | 845 |
| 1924, ignoring change in numbers, | | | |
| percentage increase | 90·6 | 112 | |
| result | 1300 | 346 | 1646 |
| effective change in numbers | +7·5% | −3·3% | |
| Hence actual wages in 1924 | 1397 | 334 | 1731 |
| Subtract 4½% for South Ireland | | | 76 |
| 1924 wage-bill, Great Britain and North Ireland | | | 1655 |

But while unemployment was reckoned as reducing earnings by 3·8 per cent. in 1911, we must allow for a reduction of 8·3 per cent. in 1924. Increased holidays without pay probably lead to a further reduction of 1 per cent. The total is therefore to be reduced by 5·5 per cent. (£91 Mn), and we have still to add £40 Mn for soldiers and sailors abroad. We thus finally obtain £1600 Mn as aggregate wages in Great Britain and North Ireland in 1924. It is suggested that there is a possible margin of error of £80 Mn, but it is believed that it is sufficient to allow ±£40 Mn, at least in comparison with 1914.

In the table these two estimates, viz. for 1911 and 1924, are the pivots. For other years the index-numbers of wages (p. 30 above), the estimates of the working class occupied (pp. 128 *seq.*), and the trade-union or national insurance unemployment statistics, are applied to obtain the two series estimated, National Wage Bill 1880–1914 and 1924–36, in the Table, p. 76.

*Note.* The change from 1911 to 1914 is that shown on p. 74. With the addition of soldiers' and sailors' wages we obtain the figures in the last column on the next page.

The diminution in the number of occupied females from 1914 to 1924 is due to the reduction in the number of domestic servants. There was a more than compensating growth of the number of clerks and other middle-class occupations.

In the following table the first column of index-numbers is repeated from p. 30 above. The second is 100, less the percentage unemployed, using the trade-union percentages till 1914 and the insurance percentages from 1924.[1] The third shows the estimated change in the number of wage-earners, based on 103·4 in 1914, a number chosen so that the product of the three index-numbers in that year should be 100. The data are the estimated numbers of wage-earners at Census dates, obtained as described in Appendix E, where middle-class occupations (including shop assistants) are subtracted from the totals occupied; between the Census dates the numbers are interpolated so as to

[1] In 1923 when both measurements of unemployment were available they gave practically identical results.

## TABLE XII

### *The National Wage-Bill,* 1880 *to* 1936

| Year | Index-numbers | | | | National wage-bill | |
|---|---|---|---|---|---|---|
| | Wages per head | Employment | Number of earners | Product aggregate wages | Excluding shop assistants (£ millions) | Including shop assistants (£ millions) |
| 1880 | 72 | 94·5 | 74·8 | 51 | 407 | 439 |
| 1881 | 72 | 96·5 | 75·7 | 53 | 421 | 453 |
| 1882 | 75 | 97·7 | 76·5 | 56 | 449 | 484 |
| 1883 | 75 | 97·4 | 77·4 | 57 | 451 | 486 |
| 1884 | 75 | 91·9 | 78·3 | 54 | 432 | 466 |
| 1885 | 73 | 90·7 | 79·2 | 52 | 419 | 452 |
| 1886 | 72 | 89·8 | 80·0 | 52 | 414 | 446 |
| 1887 | 73 | 92·4 | 80·9 | 55 | 437 | 471 |
| 1888 | 75 | 95·1 | 81·7 | 58 | 467 | 504 |
| 1889 | 80 | 97·9 | 82·6 | 65 | 518 | 558 |
| 1890 | 83 | 97·9 | 83·5 | 68 | 543 | 586 |
| 1891 | 83 | 96·5 | 84·4 | 68 | 541 | 583 |
| 1892 | 83 | 93·7 | 85·3 | 66 | 531 | 573 |
| 1893 | 83 | 92·5 | 86·1 | 66 | 529 | 571 |
| 1894 | 83 | 93·1 | 86·9 | 67 | 537 | 579 |
| 1895 | 83 | 94·2 | 87·7 | 69 | 549 | 592 |
| 1896 | 83 | 96·7 | 88·5 | 71 | 569 | 614 |
| 1897 | 84 | 96·7 | 89·4 | 73 | 581 | 626 |
| 1898 | 87 | 97·2 | 90·2 | 76 | 610 | 658 |
| 1899 | 89 | 98·0 | 91·0 | 79 | 635 | 685 |
| 1900 | 94 | 97·5 | 91·8 | 84 | 674 | 726 |
| 1901 | 93 | 96·7 | 92·7 | 83 | 667 | 719 |
| 1902 | 91 | 96·0 | 93·5 | 82 | 654 | 705 |
| 1903 | 91 | 95·3 | 94·3 | 82 | 655 | 706 |
| 1904 | 89 | 94·0 | 95·1 | 80 | 637 | 686 |
| 1905 | 89 | 95·0 | 95·9 | 81 | 649 | 700 |
| 1906 | 91 | 96·4 | 96·7 | 85 | 679 | 732 |
| 1907 | 96 | 96·3 | 97·5 | 90 | 723 | 779 |
| 1908 | 94 | 92·2 | 98·4 | 85 | 682 | 736 |
| 1909 | 94 | 92·3 | 99·2 | 86 | 688 | 742 |
| 1910 | 94 | 95·3 | 100·0 | 90 | 717 | 774 |
| 1911 | 95 | 97·0 | 100·9 | 93 | 744 | 802 |
| 1912 | 98 | 96·8 | 101·7 | 97 | 772 | 832 |
| 1913 | 99 | 97·9 | 102·5 | 99 | 795 | 857 |
| 1914 | 100 | 96·7 | 103·4 | 100 | 800 | 863 |

TABLE XII (*cont.*)

| | | | | | | Excluding South Ireland |
|---|---|---|---|---|---|---|
| 1924 | 194 | 89·7 | 107·4 | 187 | 1480 | 1600 |
| 1925 | 196 | 88·7 | 108·1 | 188 | 1490 | 1610 |
| 1926* | 195 | — | 108·8 | — | — | — |
| 1927 | 196 | 90·3 | 109·6 | 194 | 1540 | 1660 |
| 1928 | 194 | 89·2 | 110·3 | 191 | 1510 | 1630 |
| 1929 | 193 | 89·6 | 111·1 | 193 | 1520 | 1640 |
| 1930 | 191 | 83·9 | 111·9 | 179 | 1430 | 1540 |
| 1931 | 189 | 78·7 | 112·7 | 167 | 1330 | 1430 |
| 1932 | 185 | 77·9 | 113·0 | 164 | 1290 | 1390 |
| 1933 | 183 | 80·1 | 113·7 | 166 | 1320 | 1420 |
| 1934 | 186 | 83·3 | 114·3 | 177 | 1400 | 1510 |
| 1935 | 191 | 84·5 | 115·2 | 186 | 1470 | 1590 |
| 1936 | 197 | 86·8 | 117·7 | 204 | 1600 | 1720 |

\* Coal stoppage; the effect on employment cannot be accurately measured.

give a smooth movement. After 1931 numbers are extrapolated on the basis of the number of persons insured in the unemployment insurance scheme (excluding agriculture). The sudden increase in 1936 might suggest that entries were abnormal in that year, but in fact the increase of the birth-rate from 1918–19 to 1920–1 accounts for the change. The improvement of employment in 1936 was sufficient to absorb the new entrants and many of the formerly unemployed. Similarly, the check in 1932 was due to the fall in the birth-rate from 1914–15 to 1916–17.

The product of these three columns, divided by 10,000, yields the index-number of the National Wage-Bill, with 100 as the number in 1914. These products are applied to the estimates of wages in 1911 (or, what comes to the same thing, in 1924), excluding shop assistants, and also including them. The former is the better based, the latter the more familiar setting. In post-war figures the inclusion is more reasonable, since they are included in the insurance figures on which the number of the working class is based. There it is assumed that changes in rates of shop assistants do not differ significantly from general changes. There is a necessary looseness in the whole treatment, but it only affects some 10 per cent. of the wages. In statements of the total national income this looseness is rectified.

The pre-war figures include the whole of Ireland; the subsequent figures include only North Ireland. It was estimated that in 1911 the part of the wage-bill from South Ireland was $4\frac{1}{2}$ per cent., or £76 Mn; but in fact the exact amount is uncertain, for the reason, among others, that it is difficult to ascertain the number of wage-earners, apart from farmers, in Irish agriculture.

# Chapter VI

## THE NATIONAL INCOME

### I. 1911 AND 1924

It is not proposed to discuss here the definition of National Income, but only to recapitulate the estimates made for the years 1911 and 1924 (refs. 45, 47), which are unfortunately out of print, and to show their relation to the Wage-Bill, as computed in the preceding pages, with some reference to the course of Income over other periods.

The basis of these estimates is the aggregation of three groups of incomes: (1) wages, (2) income assessed to income-tax, (3) intermediate income, that is, income not falling into the first two classes.

The details of assessment to income-tax have changed very frequently, but a comparison rectified for such changes throughout the years 1842–3 to 1913–14 is available in *British Incomes and Property*, pp. 318–19 (ref. 83). For the year 1911 the total £962 Mn was found for the incomes of all persons in the United Kingdom whose annual income from all sources was over the then exemption limit, £160.

The corresponding total for 1924 was estimated as follows (ref. 45, pp. 16–18):

The fiscal year 1924–5 corresponded as closely as possible to the calendar year 1924, except for profits under Schedule D, which were then averaged over preceding years. Since 1924 was a more prosperous year than those immediately preceding, it was necessary to increase the 1924–5 assessment in this Schedule by £153 Mn.

A second adjustment was made so as to exclude incomes under £150, the exemption limit for earned incomes, since for unearned incomes the limit was £135, and those between £135 and £150 are more conveniently included throughout as 'intermediate' income.

The starting-point of the estimate is the total of what is termed 'actual income' by the income-tax authorities. This is the 'gross income', which includes all income brought under review, less income totally exempt, income of charities, income on foreign accounts, and allowances for wear and tear, etc. Actual income in 1924–5 was £2401 Mn.[1] But for the purpose of computing National Income we ought to include the income of charities.

The final estimate was as follows:

*Income of persons assessed to income-tax, United Kingdom, 1924*

|  |  | £ millions |
|---|---:|---:|
| Actual Income |  | 2401 |
| Add |  |  |
|    Rectification for Schedule D | 153 |  |
|    Charities | 30 |  |
|    War loan, etc., tax-free | 25 |  |
|    Evasion | 75 |  |
|  |  | + 283 |
| Subtract |  |  |
|    Over-assessment | 50 |  |
|    Intermediate income | 35 |  |
|    Wages | 343 |  |
|    Income belonging to foreigners | 25 |  |
|  |  | – 453 |
| Net actual income |  | 2231 |

The questions of over-assessment and evasion are discussed in *British Incomes and Property*, pp. 178–203 and 234. These items, as well as non-taxed income and income belonging to foreigners, are subject to error, amounting to perhaps ± £20 Mn.

The problem of estimating intermediate income involves the factors of numbers and average income. An essential element of security in income estimates is the inclusion of every person who has an income; it is often indifferent under which category he comes; for the total it does not matter whether he is classed as wage-earner or intermediate. The procedure is to find from

[1] The preliminary estimate for 1924–5 which was used was only £2310 Mn, and the wages included were £290 Mn. The final estimate here taken is £2402 Mn, with wages £343 Mn. Corresponding adjustments have been made in pp. 83–4 below. The net increase is £38 Mn.

the Population Census the number of occupied persons not classed as wage-earners, estimate in each occupational group how many receive less than the limit of exemption from income-tax (£160 in 1911, £150 in 1924), and estimate the average incomes. We then have to add income from property, most of which is reviewed and exempted by the income-tax authorities, so that a fairly accurate estimate can be given. Some control of the numbers is possible by adding the number of persons assessed to tax, for which from time to time some data are available, and comparing the total with estimates from the Census of the number of persons, occupied or not, who have incomes.

The final estimate for 1924 (ref. 47, p. 26) was:

*Occupied persons other than wage-earners. United Kingdom*
Incomes under £150

| | Males | | Females | |
|---|---|---|---|---|
| | Number (thou-sands) | Aggre-gate income (£ millions) | Number (thou-sands) | Aggre-gate income (£ millions) |
| Salaried | 344 | 30 | 781 | 71 |
| Farmers | 240 | 24 | 20 | 2 |
| Employers | 40 | 5 | 60 | 6 |
| Independent workers | 220 | 26 | 300 | 26 |
| Total | 844 | 85 | 1161 | 105 |

For comparison with 1911 we have (p. 46):

Intermediate income

| | 1911 Including South Ireland (£ millions) | 1924 Excluding South Ireland (£ millions) |
|---|---|---|
| Salaries | 84 | 101 |
| Other earnings | 180 | 89 |
| Dividends, etc. | 50 | 77 |
| Total | 314 | 267 |

For salaries a questionnaire was sent to principal employers by a Committee of the British Association in 1911 (see *Journal of the Royal Statistical Society*, 1910–11, pp. 17–66 (ref. 26)) and by the authors of *The National Income* in 1924. Adequate returns were received from public authorities, bankers and other bodies, and an illuminating sample from commercial and industrial firms. In each case the question was 'How many salaried males and females are employed, and what are the numbers and salaries of those who receive less than £160 or £150?' The answers, applied to the whole numbers engaged in the groups in the United Kingdom, led to the estimates of salaries in the table just given.

For farmers the numbers of agricultural holdings of different sizes were tabulated, and it was estimated how many and what incomes were included in the income-tax returns. A check was available in the estimates of the value of the whole produce of agriculture, which must be equal to the sum of agricultural wages and incomes.

For the small class of employers, with less than the exemption limit, it was necessary to include a small rather arbitrary sum.

For independent workers only rough assumptions were possible, which are described for 1911 in the *Statistical Journal* (ref. 26).

Consideration of the various numbers and amounts involved in the different groups led to the judgment that in 1924 the estimated income might be £10 Mn in excess to £20 Mn in defect of the fact.

Some items of income are not so far included. War pensions and old-age pensions are the incomes of the recipients. (Sums given from public relief or charity are excluded.) The sickness and unemployment funds come partly from the State, partly from workers' and partly from employers' contributions. In the estimates the State's contribution was ignored as being a transfer of, not an addition to, income. The workers' contribution is subtractive from wages, but comes back as benefit.

The employers' contribution has not been counted in their income, and comes in as benefit.

We have so far

### United Kingdom. National Income

|  | 1911 Including South Ireland (£ millions) | 1924 Excluding South Ireland (£ millions) |
|---|---|---|
| Above exemption limit other than wages | 962 | 2232* |
| Intermediate income | 314 | 267 |
| Wages | 802 | 1600 |
| War and old-age pensions | 20 | 93 |
| Insurance funds | 0 | 35 |
|  | 2098 | 4227 |
| Subtract payment to the United States less reparations | 0 | 24 |
| Subtract 4 per cent. of home produced income to eliminate South Ireland | 76 | 0 |
| Disposable income in Great Britain and North Ireland | 2022 | 4203 |

\* £25 Mn, income belonging to foreigners but assessed to tax, is excluded here instead of being subtracted at the end as on p. 46 (ref. 47). The £38 Mn described on p. 80 (note) as additive from the revised statement of actual income is included.

By disposable income is to be understood the total of incomes that comes into the possession of individuals or corporations in the United Kingdom (less South Ireland) and can be disposed of in private or public expenditure or saved at their choice. Of the aggregate income part is transferred before expenditure. Some decision has to be made of the treatment of rates and taxes. Among rates that part which is paid on business premises has not been included as income, since it is deductive as expenses. Rates paid on other premises and taxes, with the exception that follows, are taken as payment for services rendered and not as transfers. The exception is the payment of interest on the national debt to holders in the United Kingdom, on the ground that this is not a payment for services rendered in the year that the interest is received. On the same ground pensions, other than those that can be considered deferred pay, subtractive in one year and additive in another, are treated as transfers. This treatment is discussed in Chapter v, ref. 47.

We have what may be termed Social Income:

|  | 1911 (£ millions) | 1924 (£ millions) |
|---|---|---|
| Disposable income | 2022 | 4203 |
| Less Pensions | 20 | 93 |
| Interest on National Debt | 14 | 268 |
| Social income | 1988 | 3842 |

Another classification yields:

|  | 1911 (£ millions) | | 1924 (£ millions) | |
|---|---|---|---|---|
| Earned: | | | | |
| Below exemption limit | 1066 | | 1790 | |
| Above | 343 | | 1080 | |
| | | 1409 | | 2870 |
| | | | less (to U.S.A.) 24 | |
| | | | | 2846 |
| From property: | | | | |
| Home produced | 475 | | 1048 | |
| From abroad, net | 194 | | 180 | |
| | | 669 | | 1228 |
| Pensions and insurance | 20 | | | 128 |
| Aggregate | | 2098 | | 4202 |

The £38 Mn included on revision has been allotted rather arbitrarily, 10 to higher salaries and 28 to home-produced income from property. It should be said that the division of income under Schedule D between profits and earnings cannot be made exactly, because among other reasons a man using his own capital does not distinguish what part is earned and what is interest. The division has been made on the same principle at both dates and in figures used below.

There is necessarily a considerable element of estimate in most of the items included in the totals. Consideration of them leads to the conclusion that we should allow a margin of ± £60 Mn to the 1911 totals and of ± £100 Mn to those of 1924. These margins of course are of a different character from the variations according to the definitions of income. Since the methods of estimate were as nearly as possible the same at the two dates, many of the difficulties are lessened in comparison. It is thought that the increase of 'disposable' income in Great Britain and Northern Ireland from 1911 to 1924 may be stated as 107 ± 5 per cent., and that of 'social' income as 93 ± 5 per cent. Per head of the population the increase is estimated at 83[1] per cent. with a similar margin.

There is no means of measuring at all exactly the fall in the purchasing power of money as applied to the expenditure of income between these dates. But when all the relevant information was considered it was estimated that the rise in prices as applicable to personal expenditure was in the neighbourhood of 90 per cent., with the conclusion that *real home-produced income per head (when duplication is eliminated) in* 1924 *did not differ appreciably from that in* 1911 (p. 56). If we include income from abroad, which actually was less in 1924 than in 1911, the real income per head is found to have fallen about 5 per cent. or rather less.

In Chapter II, p. 30, it was estimated that 'real' wages per head increased in the ratio 97 to 111, or 14 per cent., in the same period. This is without allowance on the one side for increased unemployment, or on the other for reduction of hours and unemployment benefit.

The proportion of aggregate wages to home-produced social income was, however, very nearly the same, 43 per cent., at both dates; this apparent discrepancy is due to increased unemployment and a diminution of the number of wage-earners relatively to the whole population. When middle-class earnings are included, it is found that all earned income was 75½ per cent. of home-produced social income in 1911, and had increased to 78 per cent. in 1924. The difference is due to the increasing numbers in the middle class, as defined on pp. 133–4 below.

Note 1. Other estimates of the National Income in 1924 are by Mr (now Sir Alfred) Flux, *Journal of the Royal Statistical Society*, 1929

[1] Slightly corrected from text (ref. 47, pp. 49–50).

(ref. 72), and by Mr C. Clark, *The National Income, 1924–31* (ref. 69). The former, mainly based on the Census of Production of 1924, leads to the estimate £3975 ±275 Mn, with the suggestion that the margin can be reduced and the result given as between £3750 and £4200 Mn. This margin includes the estimates in the text. Mr Clark states the income comparable with the 'social' income in the text (£3840 ± 100 Mn) at £3586 Mn, with no margin of possible error. Owing to the approximate nature of several of the estimates of numbers and incomes, and the different lines of approach, it is not surprising that two estimates should differ by 10 per cent. The differences are analysed in *Economica*, 1933, pp. 138–42. The only important discrepancy is in the *number* of incomes, especially of those from wages. Mr Clark does not account for all the persons stated to be occupied in the Population Census of 1921; his numbers are obtained by building up from the insurance figures, with hazardous estimates. He returns to the question in his later book, *National Income and Outlay*, 1937 (ref. 70), and does not modify the estimate in this respect except to lower the wages slightly. Since the material and methods are adequately described in the references here given, it is not necessary to discuss them minutely. On the principle that all persons apparently having incomes must be accounted for, I am not prepared to accept the lower estimate for 1924.

For comparative purposes with 1911 a reduction would be necessary in both estimates if in either, and Mr Clark's reckoning of the change between 1911 and 1924 cannot be accepted, unless he makes a new estimate for the earlier date. In any case, in the following pages the comparisons with income from 1880 onwards are hardly affected by the doubt as to the absolute income at the basic date.

*Note* 2. I have thought it best not to include any study of the distribution of income between individuals. The statistics for super-tax payers are well known and easily accessible, and the reader may be referred to Sir Josiah Stamp's study in the *Journal of the Royal Statistical Society* (ref. 84). For 'intermediate incomes', which overlap wages, the data are quite fragmentary; they are given for what they are worth in the British Association's Committee Report and in *The National Income 1924*. The amount of income between the limits of income-tax exemption and super-tax can be estimated reasonably well, but the number of taxpayers is not known. Mr L. R. Connor's paper in the *Statistical Journal*, 1928, illuminates the difficulties and suggests some solutions. I have not published any estimates for post-war years, and those for earlier dates were given rather as showing the results of various hypotheses than as definitive. They are to be found in the *Evidence to the Select Committee on Income Tax* of 1906, and in articles in *The Nineteenth Century*, May

1910, and the *Quarterly Journal of Economics*, February 1914 (ref. 31). Part of the latter is quoted in *The Change in the Distribution of the National Income* (ref. 46).

## II. 1924 TO 1935

It is not within the plan of this book to make a complete esti-mate of income subsequent to 1924. The major constituents can be stated on the same basis as before for every year till 1935; but the changes in salaries are not known, and there have been two variations in the income-tax exemption limit, which complicate any computation of the amount of intermediate income. The variations of total income, apart from the fall during the depression of 1929 to 1932 and the subsequent re-covery, have been so small as to be dominated by these un-knowns. Also during a depression and recovery the element of approximation is greater than when trade is more stable.

The major constituents are as follows:

| Year | Wages (£ millions) | Actual income (£ millions) | | |
|---|---|---|---|---|
| | | Total | Wages | Net |
| 1924 | 1600 | 2401 | 343* | 2058 |
| 1925 | 1600 | 2337 | 243 | 2094 |
| 1926 | 1590 | 2337 | 196 | 2141 |
| 1927 | 1660 | 2416 | 285 | 2131 |
| 1928 | 1630 | 2494 | 284 | 2210 |
| 1929 | 1640 | 2531 | 290 | 2241 |
| 1930 | 1530 | 2497 | 269 | 2228 |
| 1931 | 1430 | 2725 | 519 | 2206 |
| 1932 | 1390 | 2554 | 486 | 2067 |
| 1933 | 1420 | 2505 | 504 | 2001 |
| 1934 | 1510 | 2616 | 518 | 2097 |
| 1935 | 1590 | 2740 | — | — |
| 1936 | 1720 | — | — | — |

* Mr Clark states that shop-assistants' wages are not included in this column (ref. 70, p. 53).

Here the first column of wages includes those of shop assistants. The next column contains the wages which are assessed to income-tax (though in fact a great part does not pay, because of the various abatements allowed). The last column is the remainder after wages are subtracted from actual income.

As in the 1924 estimate the fiscal year 1924–5 is taken as equivalent to the calendar year 1924, and similarly for subsequent years.

In 1925–6 the exemption limit for earned incomes was raised from £150 to £162, while that for unearned incomes was left at £135. In 1931–2 the exemption limit for earned incomes was lowered to £125 and that for unearned to £100. The effect of the first change is masked in the figures by the coal stoppage and the resultant loss of wages and income in 1926. In 1927 it appears as a greater amount of wages to be subtracted from 'actual' income. The effect on small salaries, which in 1924 were estimated as aggregating only £100 Mn, can hardly have exceeded a sum which is practically negligible in comparison with the whole national income.

The alteration in 1931–2 is more serious. As regards unearned income, however, it merely transfers part of the dividends, etc., formerly accredited to small incomes to those included among the larger. Of earned incomes the bulk is wages, which appeared in the subtractive column in the above table, and the classification and figures used are not affected. As regards earned intermediate income there is a change, and part of the earnings and profits, estimated at £190 Mn in 1924, is after 1931 included in actual income above the exemption limit. For considering the amount involved we have the estimate (ref. 47, p. 27) that in 1924 2,000,000 persons other than wage-earners had incomes under £150 aggregating £190 Mn, with an average of £95. Since 1924 there has been some increase in numbers of the persons in the occupations affected and probably some reduction of average earnings. The opinion may be provisionally hazarded that on the same definitions as in 1924 the earned income has been reduced from £190 Mn under £150 to between £140 Mn and £170 Mn under £125 in 1934.

Of the various adjustments made for 1924 to the income-tax total to estimate income according to the definition required, that for adjustment of the year of profits has become unim-

portant since 1927–8, when Schedule D was altered to a one
year's basis. For subsequent years we have only to add income
of charities (p. 80) and whatever corresponds to tax-free
war loan, evasions, over-assessment and income of foreigners,
which came to £100 Mn less £75 Mn = £25 Mn in 1924.

We have the following comparison:

|  | 1924 (£ millions) | 1934 (£ millions) |
|---|---|---|
| Assessed income less wages | 2058 | 2098 |
| Adjustment for year | 153 | 0 |
| Charities | 30 | 42 |
| Evasion, etc. less over-assessment, etc. | 25 | 25 |
| Dividends below exemption limit | 77 | *77* |
| Earnings below exemption limit | 190 | *155 ± 15* |
| Wages | 1600 | 1510 |
| War pensions | 69 | 44 |
| Employers' contributions to insurance funds | 35 | *50* |
| Old-age pensions | 24 | 21 |
| *Subtract adjustment for exemption limit* | *35* | *0* |
| Aggregate income | 4226 | 4022 ± 30 |

The figures in italics are unverified estimates.

Both totals need adjustment for income of the Government
from reparation and other sources less outpayments, and also
for transfers (pensions and national debt interest, see pp. 83–4),
to obtain social income. The totals as given represent approximately the money coming into the hands of individuals.

It is suggested that the doubtful elements introduced since
1924 may amount to ± £30 Mn. This is in addition to the
5 per cent. margin allowed for the 1924 estimate, but the errors
and uncertainties then included are of similar sign and dimen-
sions at both dates.

Thus total income fell about 5 per cent. from 1924 to 1934,
while population increased about 4 per cent. Per head in 1924
the income so reckoned was £90 to £100; in 1934, £80 to £90.
With the increase in prosperity since 1934 it must have ap-
proached the 1924 level per head at the time of writing.

Real income per head was no doubt greater in 1934 than in
1924, since the cost of living index had fallen 20 per cent.,
while average money income as here reckoned had fallen only

10 per cent. It will be remembered that on p. 30 above it was estimated that 'real' wages per head had increased about 19 per cent. (111 : 132) in the period, but this did not allow for increased unemployment; the wage-bill is practically the same proportion of income as reckoned above at both dates.

It should be emphasised that the statistics now given are only a rough estimate of the movement of income. A great deal of detail is to be found in Mr C. Clark's recent book, *National Income and Outlay*. He uses different definitions and estimates, and in fact finds an increase in aggregate income in the ten years, mainly since his estimate of wages differs from that here used. The reasons for this are discussed in *Economica*, August 1937, p. 351.

## III. 1880 TO 1913

From the difficulty of choosing the definition of income and of assembling and combining the relevant data for the estimates of 1911 and 1924, it will be expected that we cannot be on very safe ground when we attempt estimates at earlier dates.

The only definite consecutive account of income is that arising from the collection of income-tax. There have been many changes in methods of assessment, but these were so exhaustively dealt with by (Sir Josiah) Stamp in *British Incomes and Property*, 1916, that we can accept his estimates of the movement of income on any unchanged definition without hesitation. The first numerical column in Table XIII shows his series for taxable income, that is, gross income less exemptions and reductions for depreciation, etc., but without subtraction of abatements for earned income, small incomes, etc.

The estimate of the total of wages has fair precision as a comparative series and within the definition adopted. The other series are the result of hazardous estimates, made by various writers. That for evasion is essentially a guess at the extent of the unobserved. It is, however, certain that some kinds of income that evaded tax in 1880 were brought into assessment in later decades, so that whatever is to be added is less in 1913

than in 1880. The problem is similar to that of estimating the
deficit in import statistics due to smuggling. There are few
commodities the smuggling of which is profitable, their maximum amount can be reasonably guessed, and the change due to
the inclusion or exclusion of commodities and to any variation
in the efficiency of the preventive service can be estimated.

The amount of income not received as wages and not
assessed to income-tax was only the subject of broad approxi-
mations before 1910, and there was no original estimate between
1883 and that date. These estimates are listed on p. 240 below.
We may take it that the estimate for 1910 was fairly precise.
The main justification for the increase estimated from 1880 to
1910 is to be found in the Population Census statistics, as discussed on pp. 127 *seq.* below. The salient figures are as follows:

*Estimates of Occupied Population of the United Kingdom*

| Year | Working class (thousands) | Middle and upper classes (thousands) | Total (thousands) |
|------|---------------------------|--------------------------------------|-------------------|
| 1881 | 11,840 | 2610 | 14,450 |
| 1891 | 12,810 | 3210 | 16,020 |
| 1901 | 13,800 | 3940 | 17,740 |
| 1911 | 14,710 | 4990 | 19,700 |

In this shop assistants are included under middle class.

The number of income-tax payers is not known, but it has
been estimated at about 620,000 for 1880 and about 1,150,000
for 1911. This leaves approximately 2,000,000 in the intermediate class in 1880 and 3,840,000 in 1911. But some of the
taxpayers are unoccupied and the figures thus roughly estimated
are not exactly those finally adopted; the increase in the number
of the intermediate class is probably even greater than here
appears.

On the basis used for the table the average income of persons
in the intermediate class is about £70 in 1880 and about £84
in 1911.

In these two uncertain columns the amounts in the intermediate years are interpolated.

TABLE XIII

*The National Income, 1880 to 1913*

| Year (average) | Income over £160 | | Intermediate income‡ (£Mn) | Wages, including shop assistants§ (£Mn) | Total (£Mn) (say) | | Percentages of total | | |
|---|---|---|---|---|---|---|---|---|---|
| | Taxable* (£Mn) | Evasion† (£Mn) | | | | | Over £160 | Intermediate | Wages |
| 1880 | 469 | 60 | 120 | 439 | 1088 | 1090 | 49 | 11 | 40 |
| 1881–5 | 489 | (62) | (139) | 468 | 1158 | 1160 | 48 | 12 | 40 |
| 1886–90 | 528 | (60) | (170) | 513 | 1271 | 1270 | 46 | 14 | 40 |
| 1891–5 | 562 | (59) | (202) | 580 | 1403 | 1400 | 44 | 14½ | 41½ |
| 1896–1900 | 664 | (59) | (233) | 662 | 1618 | 1620 | 45 | 14 | 41 |
| 1901–5 | 741 | (55) | (265) | 703 | 1764 | 1760 | 45 | 15 | 40 |
| 1906–10 | 830 | (47) | (296) | 753 | 1926 | 1930 | 45½ | 15½ | 39 |
| 1911 | 907 | (40) | 314 | 802 | 2063 | 2060‖ | 45 | 15 | 40 |
| 1912 | 951 | (38) | [330] | 832 | 2151 | 2150 | 46 | 15 | 39 |
| 1913 | 985 | 37 | [340] | 857 | 2219 | 2220 | 46 | 15½ | 38½ |

* Taxable income over £160 is taken from Stamp's *British Income and Property*, pp. 318–19. The Fiscal Year, such as 1881–2, is taken as corresponding to the Calendar Year 1880.

† Stamp discusses the question of evasion owing to under-assessment of profits and untaxed income from abroad. From the estimates of various authorities I deduced £60 Mn in 1880 and £37 Mn in 1913 as reasonable estimates (ref. 44, p. 9). For intermediate years I have assumed a regularly falling percentage of taxable income under Schedule D (Profits, etc.).

‡ Intermediate income in 1911 is as explained on p. 82 above. For 1880 the rough estimate £120 Mn is taken as explained in the note below (p. 140), less an arbitrary £10 Mn, since shop assistants are excluded. Between these dates regular arithmetic progression is assumed. For 1912 and 1913 the same percentage of column 1 as in 1911 is assumed.

§ The wage estimate is from p. 76 above.

‖ To obtain continuity part of the income for 1911, as given on p. 83, is omitted, viz. £20 Mn pensions and £26 Mn unallotted agricultural income; on the other hand the estimate for incomes over £160 is about £11 Mn greater here, owing to slight changes in estimates of evasion, etc. Thus £35 Mn should be added to reconcile the estimates, but it is quite doubtful what should be added (if anything) in earlier years.

It will be realised that the uniform division at £160 is only made because the data arise in that form. In 1913 it reached considerably further down the incomes than in 1880, since at the latter date average money incomes were some 40 per cent. higher than at the former. An attempt was made to get a more uniform basis for comparison in *The Change in the Distribution of the National Income* (ref. 46, p. 10), by estimating the amount of income in 1913 above £225, the limit as raised in proportion to income, or rather on the basis that the number of payers should have increased at the same rate as the occupied population. This would transfer about 380,000 persons, but only £75 Mn income, from the upper to the intermediate class, so that intermediate income so reckoned would be about £415 Mn.

The separation of wages from other kinds of income corresponds with usual ideas, but in fact the intermediate class is very largely recruited from working-class parents, and there is no logical division between the nature and amount of payments for so-called manual labour and for clerical and administrative work; there is a considerable margin where the classification is arbitrary. The increase in the whole number occupied has been greater than that of wage-earners, and this is the chief reason why wages have been a slightly diminishing part of total income. The relation of all earnings to total income is considered below (pp. 95–7).

We get another view from Table XIV (p. 94). Money income per head of the whole population rose from about £32 in 1880 to about £49 in 1913,[1] that is, in the ratio 65 to 100, or about 55 per cent. Reckoned per occupied person average money income rose from about £76 to £110, or about 45 per cent. With the change in age distribution the proportion of occupied to all persons had increased. In the same period average wages or earnings per annum had risen in the smaller ratio 73 : 100 or about 38 per cent. The relative loss dates from about the year 1900, after which wages apparently failed to keep up completely with rising prices.

The difficulties of making adjustment for change of prices are even greater for non-wage incomes than for wages, for the

[1] The basis is aggregate income, without reduction, or, what comes to nearly the same thing, 'social' income, see p. 84.

records of retail prices, principally of food and rent, are not directly applicable to the expenditure of the larger incomes. Fortunately the height both of retail and of wholesale prices was nearly the same in 1913 as in 1880, and it is the intermediate fall and rise that is less certain. The table shows the result of correction of all money by the cost of living index discussed above (p. 30). The relative courses of wages and of all income are naturally unaffected, and that of wages has already been discussed. When figures equivalent to these were first published

TABLE XIV

*Real Income and Wages, 1880 to 1913*

| Year (av.) | United Kingdom | | Income per head of | | Index-numbers | | | | | |
|---|---|---|---|---|---|---|---|---|---|---|
| | | | | | Income | | | | Real | |
| | Population (thousands) | Occupied (thousands) | Population £ | Occupied £ | Per head | Per occupied | Wage rates | Cost of living | Income per occupied person | Wages per earner |
| 1880 | 3460 | 1429 | 31·5 | 76·1 | 65 | 69 | 73 | 103 | 67 | 70 |
| 1881–5 | 3546 | 1476 | 32·7 | 78·5 | 67 | 72 | 75 | 97 | 74 | 77 |
| 1886–90 | 3675 | 1553 | 34·5 | 81·2 | 71 | 74 | 77 | 87 | 85 | 89 |
| 1891–5 | 3848 | 1636 | 36·4 | 85·8 | 75 | 78 | 84 | 85½ | 91 | 98 |
| 1896–1900 | 4034 | 1719 | 40·2 | 94·1 | 82½ | 85½ | 88 | 85 | 100 | 104 |
| 1901–5 | 4220 | 1813 | 41·7 | 97·3 | 85½ | 88½ | 92 | 89½ | 99 | 103 |
| 1906–10 | 4409 | 1914 | 43·8 | 100·6 | 90 | 91½ | 95 | 92 | 100 | 103 |
| 1911 | 4522 | 1967 | 45·6 | 104·9 | 93½ | 95½ | 96 | 95 | 100 | 100 |
| 1912 | 4543 | 1987 | 47·3 | 108·3 | 97 | 98½ | 99 | 98 | 100 | 100 |
| 1913 | 4565 | 2006 | 48·8 | 110·1 | 100 | 100 | 100 | 100 | 100 | 100 |

they were accepted, if at all, with surprise, for it was generally believed from superficial observation that people were well off in the years immediately before the war in comparison with earlier years. Per head of the population there was an increase of real income, so measured, of about 4 per cent. in ten years, but per occupied person the statistics are convincingly against any average increase, and the slight relative loss in wages is not enough to account for any marked change in distribution which would lead to the emergence of an enlarged wealthy class. The explanation of the discrepancy between appearance and the estimated statistical facts may lie in a changed habit of expenditure on the part of the well-to-do, in the direction of more display and more prominence to their doings in the press. If it had been found that a smaller proportion was saved in those years than before, the same impression would have been given of there being more free money for extravagance, but in fact investment abroad had increased in that period; it is not known how much there was at home.

Another explanation, however, may be found in the fact that while money income rose prices rose as much. Up till about 1900 the 'terms of trade' were in our favour; prices of imports had fallen more or risen less rapidly than those of exports. From about 1900 the movements were more nearly parallel; in particular the advantage of cheapening imported food was lost.[1] While it was more difficult in fact to increase real income, the feeling of having more money without a close observation of prices may have led to the appearance and fact of increased luxurious or free expenditure.

For completeness we should refer to the estimates of total earnings as compared with income from property.

The figures for the years 1911 and 1924 (*National Income*, 1924, pp. 46–52) are given on the next page.

Here pensions are old-age and war pensions. Insurance is the amount contributed by employers.

Earned income is used in the sense taken by the Income-Tax Commissioners, and includes the whole income derived by the employment of one's own capital. In 1911 there was a differential tax in favour of earned income, and the amount assessed at the lower rate is known. For 1924 it was necessary to make a more detailed estimate from other data.

On this basis total earned income was 74 per cent. of aggre-

[1] See Taussig, *Economic Journal*, 1925, pp. 1–10 (ref. 85); Beveridge, *Economica*, 1924, pp. 1 *seq.* (ref. 66) and the references there given.

gate income originating at home in 1911, 71 per cent. in 1924. But if we subtract transferred income (see p. 84 above) to obtain 'social' income, the movement is reversed; the percentages become 75½ in 1911 and 78 in 1924.

| | 1911 Including South Ireland (£ millions) | | 1924 Excluding South Ireland (£ millions) | |
|---|---|---|---|---|
| Earned income: | | | | |
| Wages | 802 | | 1600 | |
| Salaries below exemption | 84 | | 101 | |
| Salaries above exemption | 130 | | 641 | |
| Farmers | 41 | | 30 | |
| Under Schedule D | 172 | | 399 | |
| Small traders, etc. | 180 | | 89 | |
| | | 1409 | | 2860 |
| Unearned income: | | | | |
| Home produced | 475 | | 1020 | |
| From abroad | 194 | | 180 | |
| | | 669 | | 1200 |
| Pensions and insurance | 20 | | 128 | |
| Total | | 2098 | | 4188 |

For earlier years the estimates were made on a different basis in *The Change in the Distribution of the National Income* (ref. 46, pp. 23–5):

| | 1880 (£ millions) | | 1913 (£ millions) | |
|---|---|---|---|---|
| Earned income: | | | | |
| Wages | 465 | | 770 | |
| Intermediate | 105 | | 315 | |
| Assessed to tax | 135 | | 270 | |
| | | 705 | | 1355 |
| Unearned income: | | | | |
| Home produced | 370 | | 610 | |
| From abroad | 50 | | 200 | |
| | | 420 | | 810 |
| Total | | 1125 | | 2165 |

On this reckoning earned income is 62½ per cent. of the total at each date. The minor differences in the totals of income here given from those in the table on p. 92 above are discussed below (p. 139). They do not lead to any significant modification of the percentages.

But there is a discrepancy between the earned income assumed under Schedule D in the 1911 and 1913 estimates. It is not now possible to reconstruct that table on the original basis. The difference appears to arise in the treatment of 'persons' as distinct from firms, companies and employees in Schedule D, and the difficulty of reconciling the amount of income taxed at the lower rate as earned with the amount found by aggregating the entries in the different Schedules. The discrepancy between the 62½ per cent. found for 1913 and the 67 per cent. (when income from abroad is included) found in the estimate made some years after for 1911 may be considered to lie to some extent in different definitions of earned as opposed to unearned income. In both estimates the main intention was to compare the proportions in different years, and care was taken to harmonise the definitions and methods over the periods so far as the changing nature of the data allowed. The evidence however suggests that the percentage for 1913 should be slightly raised, while that for 1880 is unchanged.

The general conclusion that there was no important change in the proportion of earned to total income between 1880 and 1913 or between 1911, 1913 and 1924 remains. There is a stability between the relations of the various classes of income considered. There is some evidence of slight variations within the first period, and it is futile to try to make any estimates during the war period and in the years immediately succeeding it.

## IV. 1860 TO 1901

In 'Tests of National Progress', *Economic Journal*, 1904, pp. 457 *seq.*, there is a table (p. 459) which gives some statistics of income and wages for the period 1860–1901. It was not intended to show total income nor the proportion that fell to wages, but to set out the movement of those parts of income which seemed to be capable of yielding comparable series over the period. Intermediate income for which there are no definite estimates was omitted. The wage totals do not differ essentially from those given on p. 76 above for the same dates; what difference there is is due to a slight revision of the wage-index and also of the numbers in the working-class population. The figures for income subject to tax were compiled prior by many years to the publication of Stamp's *British Income and Property*; the method of computing them is described on pp. 458, 460; they follow very nearly the same course as the taxable income Stamp gives with an allowance for evasion, and it has seemed best not to try to doctor them in the light of later knowledge. But it is necessary to explain that attention was paid to the change in the exemption limit from £100 to £150 in 1877 and to £160 in 1895. Over the whole period the rise in average income per payer and average wages had risen in nearly the same proportion as the limit, viz. 60 per cent. The increase in the limit was taken as rising continuously and adjustments were made so as to estimate income above this rising limit, implicitly leaving any lower incomes to the intermediate class. The adjustments were in most years trifling, and the original figures and the details are given or described in the article. The following table is compiled from the original with an additional column showing the percentage that wages form of the income included.

The quinquennia are broken at 1880 so as to afford easy comparison with the completed account on p. 92 above.

The index for income per head of the population is obtained by dividing the totals of income-tax income and wages by the number of the population of the United Kingdom and expressing the series as percentages of its value in 1901.

Sauerbeck's index-numbers of wholesale prices were used to correct for the changing value of money. It is argued below (p. 122) that when comparison is possible at later dates they form a good approximation to the movements of the cost of living index-number.

It is seen that money income increased faster than the population in the first two decades included, was then checked for twenty years, and finally rose rapidly. When the change of prices is taken into account, the whole rise is more considerable, and the check, after the inflation of 1873–4, much less marked.

The proportion of wages to total income thus reckoned (that is, excluding intermediate income) varied between 48 and 43 per cent., falling gradually at first and finally recovering. There is no means of telling how intermediate income moved,

TABLE XV

*Income-tax Income, Wages and Prices, 1860 to 1901*

| Year (average) | Wages £Mn | Income £Mn | Wages and income | | Sauer-beck price-index | Quo-tient of income and wages by prices | % wages of in-come and wages |
|---|---|---|---|---|---|---|---|
| | | | £Mn | Index per head of popu-lation | | | |
| 1860–4 | 306 | 336 | 642 | 60 | 144 | 42 | 48 |
| 1865–9 | 346 | 407 | 753 | 68 | 143 | 48 | 46 |
| 1870–4 | 430 | 515 | 945 | 82 | 148 | 55 | 45½ |
| 1875–9 | 451 | 552 | 1003 | 83 | 130 | 63 | 45 |
| 1880 | 440 | 560 | 1000 | 80 | 126 | 63 | 44 |
| 1881–5 | 457 | 582 | 1039 | 81 | 114 | 71 | 44 |
| 1886–90 | 495 | 614 | 1169 | 83 | 100 | 83 | 43 |
| 1891–5 | 557 | 639 | 1196 | 86 | 95 | 91 | 48 |
| 1896–1900 | 647 | 737 | 1384 | 95 | 94 | 101 | 45 |
| 1901 | 705 | 800 | 1505 | 100 | 100 | 100 | 47 |

nor whether the proportion of earnings other than wages changed. The movement of this percentage is significantly affected by the assumptions about the moving exemption limit. Generally it would be unwise to base further arguments on the fall in the proportion so computed prior to 1880. It will be seen that if we insert rising figures for intermediate income from 1880 onwards we get a nearly constant proportion of wages to total.

In brief, I do not think that the statistics are sufficient for any fine measurements of income, earnings or wages prior to 1880; there is indeed sufficient uncertainty after that date.

7-2

# Appendix A

## NOTES ON THE WAGE CENSUSES OF
## THE UNITED KINGDOM

General enquiries about wages and earnings have been made by the Board of Trade (1886), the Labour Department (1906) and the Ministry of Labour (1924, 1928, 1931 and 1935). These differ in completeness and method. In every case the returns were voluntary and so covered only part of each industry, and they excluded small workshops, outworkers, shop assistants and agriculture. Only that of 1886 had any information about coal-mining or domestic servants.

Statistics for agriculture and for coal-mining of a general kind can, however, be obtained from other sources.

It may be held that the voluntary basis of the returns does not seriously disturb the results even for one date, and still less for comparison between two dates. For in the developed industries there can be little variation between the wages paid in one industry in one district, and the possible reluctance of firms whose wages were low to make returns can only have affected the average slightly. For comparison the bias, if it exists, would be even less important. This consideration of course does not apply to cases where classes of workers were included in one Census and not in another. The disturbing factor that the returns came in different proportions from different industries can be rectified by re-weighting the industries. In fact, re-weighting, which has been applied to each Census, is found to make very little difference to the results. For the 1906 Census no general report was published, since it was never completed.

The nature of the information obtained in the 1886 Census is described in detail in the writer's *Elements of Statistics*, 5th or 6th edition, pp. 30–6. The rates of wages paid or of average piece-earnings in a normal week without over-time were asked for each occupation in each industry in each locality. Also the total wages

paid in the year 1885 were recorded. An attempt was made to describe
the distribution of wages by the assumption that the wages for the
same occupation in one district fell in the same five-shilling grade
for all operatives, distinguishing men, women, boys and girls from
each other. The result cannot be minutely exact, but it is sufficient
for broad generalisations.

In 1906 (see *loc. cit.* pp. 36–7) the same details were obtained with
the addition of the averages of actual earnings, whether for the
normal week or as the result of over- or short-time. The averages
over all on the two bases only differed by 1 per cent., the complete
earnings being the higher. Complete tables of the distribution of
earnings, shilling by shilling, are included for each industry—the only
ones in existence. More detail was given of the numbers employed,
and the annual wage-bills were recorded; but coal and railways as
well as agriculture were excluded.

The post-War Censuses were less elaborate. The results for 1924
are published in the *Ministry of Labour Gazette*, beginning in June
1926; a summary is to be found in the issue of July 1927, pp. 250–2,
with an addendum in September, p. 330. The average week's
earnings for each industry as a whole are stated for one week in each
quarter of 1924, males being distinguished from females but not
adults from juveniles. Information is also given about normal and
actual hours of work. Reference is made to other Reports on
earnings on railways and in coal-mines, but there is nothing about
agriculture. The investigation was undertaken so as to be of use in
conjunction with the Census of Production of the same date.

The investigation of 1928 was made to afford comparison with
that of 1924, and the results are given in the *Ministry of Labour
Gazette*, October to December 1929. Except that the earnings were
ascertained for one week only, the enquiry was similar to the previous one.

The enquiry in 1931 was again connected with a Census of Production. Except that small firms are separated from large, the data
for earnings were as before, but for hours instead of giving tables of
the hours actually worked, information is only available about short-
time; since over-time has been found to be considerable whenever it
has been recorded, this seriously affects the use of this Census for

estimating earnings for a normal week's work, which is possible in the other Censuses.

The use of these Censuses in relation to the Census of Production may be seen in articles by F. Brown in *Economica*, 1928 (ref. 68), 'Expenses of Production in Great Britain', and by G. L. Schwartz in *Memorandum of the London and Cambridge Economic Service*, No. 26, 'Output, Employment and Wages in Industry in the United Kingdom, 1924'.

The Census of 1935, taken for use with the Census of Production of the same date, is published in the *Ministry of Labour Gazette*, February to May 1937. This is more detailed than the previous accounts, since it separates men over 21 from youths, and women over 18 from girls. Considerable detail is given of the normal hours in each industry, and of the amount of over- and short-time, so that it is possible to compute earnings appropriate to the normal week as well as actual earnings.

It is to be noticed that since 1906 we have no data for the distribution of wages according to their amount amongst individuals, but only averages.

Since the movement of wage-rates from 1924 to 1935 was small, in all a fall of about 5 per cent., it is to be expected that all consistent comparisons of the data will give nearly the same general results, whatever system of combination is employed. There are five methods of weighting, each of which has been tested. (i) We may take the numbers as they stand and assume that the proportion of returns for each industry is sufficiently near the numbers actually employed in the whole industry to give the average with sufficient accuracy for all industries together. (ii) Or we may take the number of males and females insured in each industrial group shown separately in the insurance statistics and weight the averages by these. (iii) Or we can subtract the number unemployed from the number insured and weight by the remainders. The last is the more accurate for computation of average actual earnings, but in the more theoretical problem of estimating average full-time wages, it is more reasonable to weight by the whole numbers insured. In each case we can adjust the earnings by the data for short-time or for over-time or both and compute the average full-time rates. (iv) Or we can use the numbers of operatives stated in the Censuses of Production, supplementing them from other sources. (v) Finally we can use the Census of Population occupation tables as alternative weights, and this is our only resource in connection with the pre-war Censuses.

In every one of these processes there is an element of approximation and of judgment. The classifications for insurance are not exactly the same as in the Wage Censuses, and these differ from one another, especially from 1886 to all subsequent dates, and from 1906 to post-war accounts. Again, the numbers insured include a considerable number of clerical workers. With the Census figures we have to combine estimates for coal-mining, railway traffic and shop workers, and agricultural labourers, for each of which the information is on a special basis. In the end we have no sufficient data for shop assistants or for domestic servants. This last group is so much one of part-time occupation for non-resident servants that in any case special treatment would be necessary.

Table XVI, p. 105, shows the results of applying various methods to the post-war Censuses. That for 1928 is omitted, since details for males and females separately are not given. It indicates an increase of actual earnings of 1 per cent. over 1924 in the industries covered by both Censuses, reduced to zero when the fall of coalminers' earnings is taken with it. In the years taken in the Table coal and railways are included.

It is seen that it is indifferent whether we apply as weights all insured or all at work for males and for females separately. But when we combine them, weighting by numbers insured gives 50·5s. for actual earnings in 1935, but weighting by numbers at work gives only 49·7s. The difference is due to the larger percentage of men unemployed than of women, so that the working force had a relatively larger number at the lower earnings.

In 1924 short-time decreased average earnings by 2½ per cent., in 1931 by nearly 4 per cent., and in 1935 by 3 per cent. It is only in 1935 that we can ascertain to what extent this was balanced by overtime. In that year, as in pre-war times so far as is known, the computed full-time earnings were the same as the actual earnings, some persons or some industries working short-time, others over-time, and the balance is nearly exact.

Within the margin of error that is intrinsic in these statistics we may take the better ascertained actual earnings as our guide for index-numbers, rather than the hypothetical earnings if all worked the normal week.

There is one further difficulty in the 1935 Census. The figures used in the computations for the table are those from firms which made separate returns for males and females. It happens that the earnings in the firms which gave only massed returns were slightly lower than those included; over all the reduction appears to be about 4d. on the week, giving an average (weighted by numbers at work from the insurance figures) of 49·3s. instead of 49·7s. For comparison with the earlier returns it seems best to take the larger figure.

These and earlier wage statistics indicate the margin of uncertainty in even the best returns. Variation of definition may make a difference of 2s. in the average. Variation of weighting has almost negligible effects. The wage-bill estimates are affected by the definition, but index-numbers need not be. The statistics are adequate for general purposes, and for showing trends and a great deal of interesting detail; but they cannot be used for establishing or measuring minute changes.

To complete our account we still have to combine with the figures in Table XVI estimates of other wage-earning occupations, namely agriculture and domestic service.

For average actual earnings in agriculture the sum 18·3s. weekly in 1906 is computed from the data in *Prices and Wages* (ref. 51, p. 170). For subsequent dates the increase to 1924 named in the *Ministry of Labour Gazette*, 1925, p. 38, has been applied for 1924, and then the changes in the county minima; the average differs from that usually published, which relates to ordinary labourers only, while those in charge of animals get more and there is a significant amount of over-time. The number engaged in agriculture has been a diminishing proportion of all male wage-earners, but the diminution has been slow and has little effect on the average for all. (See also Appendix C, p. 113 and *Journal of the Royal Statistical Society*, 1937, pp. 615 *seq.*)

It is not known how far earnings of domestic servants, including the value of food and room, differ from the general average for all women, but there seems to be no evidence that there has been any change in the relationship between these and other women's and girls' earnings in the thirty years, at least of a significance that would affect the general average. But the number of females occupied is a greater proportion of the population than appears in the Table. Among wage-earners the proportion of females was probably less in 1924 than in 1906, as may be judged from the

TABLE XVI

*Results of the Wage Censuses of 1924, 1931 and 1935*

Manual Industries covered by Unemployment Insurance together with Railways

| Year | Males | | | | Females | | | | All persons | |
|---|---|---|---|---|---|---|---|---|---|---|
| | Numbers (in thousands) | | Av. earnings (*s.* per week) | | Numbers (in thousands) | | Av. earnings (*s.* per week) | | Av. earnings (*s.* per week) | |
| | In-sured | At work | Actual | Full-time | In-sured | At work | Actual | Full-time | Actual | Full-time |
| 1924 | 7490 | — | 57·6 | 58·9 | 2142 | — | 27·5 | 28·4 | 50·9 | 52·1 |
| | — | 6619 | 57·6 | 58·9 | — | 1936 | 27·5 | 28·4 | 50·7 | 52·0 |
| 1931 | 7654 | — | 55·3 | 57·3 | 2400 | — | 26·8 | 28·0 | 48·5 | 50·4 |
| | — | 5775 | 55·7 | 57·7 | — | 1927 | 26·9 | 28·1 | 48·5 | 50·4 |
| 1935 | 7916 | — | 56·6 | a 58·3 b 56·6 | 2304 | — | 27·3 | a 28·0 b 27·2 | 50·5 | a 52·0 b 50·5 |
| | — | 6492 | 56·9 | a 58·6 b 56·8 | — | 2092 | 27·3 | a 28·0 b 27·2 | 49·7 | a 51·2 b 49·6 |

Average earnings are obtained by applying to earnings in each of about ninety industries (i) the numbers insured in July of the relevant year, (ii) these numbers less the unemployed in the month of the Census (October). For railways the numbers reported in the Railway Returns are used.

Actual earnings in each industry are those published for males and females separately in the Reports of the Censuses. 'Full-time' earnings are computed in 1924 and 1931 by applying the data for short-time in the Reports. For 1935 (*a*) gives the results from the short-time data, while (*b*) gives the results of applying also the over-time data. There is no material for computation (*b*) in 1931, and that in 1924 is incomplete and unsatisfactory.

The averages for 'All persons' are obtained by combining the earnings and numbers in the previous columns.

statistics in Appendix E. But in 1931 and in 1935 the earlier proportion was restored, owing to the fact that women suffered less
from unemployment than did men.

The effect of various hypotheses is shown in the following little
table. There it is seen that very little depends for the final index on
these proportions of agriculturists to other males, or of females to
males.

*Average earnings (in shillings)*

| Males | 1906 | 1924 | 1931 | 1935 |
|---|---|---|---|---|
| Actual earnings | | | | |
| Industry (Table XI) | 27·0 | 57·6 | 55·7 | 56·9 |
| Agriculture (p. 113)[1] | 16·7 | 28·7 | 31·9 | 32·5 |
| Combined | | | | |
| Proportion    8 : 1 | 25·9 | 54·4 | 53·1 | 54·2 |
| „           11 : 1 | 26·2 | 55·2 | 53·7 | 54·9 |
| Adopted | 25·9 | 54·4 | 53·7 | 54·7 |
| Males | 25·9 | 54·4 | 53·7 | 54·7 |
| Females (Table XI) | 11·8 | 27·5 | 26·9 | 27·3 |
| Combined | | | | |
| Proportion   7 : 3 | 21·8 | 46·3 | 45·7 | 46·5 (a) |
| „      72 : 28 in 1924 | — | 46·9 | — | — (b) |
| Index-numbers | — | 100 | 98½ | 100 (a) |
|  | — | 100 | 97 | 99 (b) |
| Index on p. 19 | — | 100 | 97 | 95 |

Thus it is clear that in 1935 the index obtained from actual
earnings reads higher than that from wage-rates as on p. 30.
This is the justification for modifying the latter as is there done.

[1] The figures of Table XI are reduced 9 per cent. to include boys.

# Appendix B

## NOTES ON SEPARATION OF THE FACTORS MAKING FOR CHANGES IN AVERAGE WAGES

The change of average wages of the whole working class over any period depends partly on the increase or decrease in the rates for a normal week, partly on the amount of unemployment, short-time and over-time, partly on changes from time- to piece-rates, and finally on the shifting of the relative numbers between occupations within an industry, and the shifting from industry to industry. (*Memorandum of the London and Cambridge Economic Service*, No. 28, p. 2 (ref. 42).) Of these factors, total unemployment is allowed for in computations of the National Wage-Bill in Chapter v. The changes within each industry are dealt with above in the working up of the Wage Censuses, where the averages for whole industries are taken, with a double reckoning for earnings in normal hours and actual earnings. There remains the factor of the influence of relative changes of the numbers in the whole industries. The analysis given in the following pages is based on 'Notes on Index Numbers', *Economic Journal*, 1928, pp. 235-7 (ref. 25). Here it is applied to the successive Wage Censuses.

*Notation.*

Number of persons in each of $m$ industries or occupations:

at first date   $N_1 \ldots N_t \ldots N_m$,

at second date   $n_1 \ldots n_t \ldots n_m$.

Average wages of these persons:

at first date   $W_1 \ldots W_t \ldots W_m$,

at second date   $w_1 \ldots w_t \ldots w_m$.

Average wage in all industries:

at first date   $\overline{W} = (W_1 N_1 + \ldots + W_t N_t + \ldots + W_m N_m)$
$$\div (N_1 + \ldots + N_t + \ldots + N_m)$$
$$= S\,(WN) \div m\overline{N},$$

where $\overline{N}$ is the average number in an industry;

at second date   $\overline{w} = S\,(wn) \div m\overline{n}.$

Forward measurement of change in average wages, the relative numbers in industries being as at first date:

$$R_1 = (w_1 N_1 + \ldots + w_t N_t + \ldots + w_m N_m)$$
$$\div (W_1 N_1 + \ldots + W_t N_t + \ldots + W_m N_m)$$
$$= S\,(wN) \div S\,(WN).$$

Backward measurement of change, the relative numbers being as at the second date:

$$R_2 = S\,(wn) \div S\,(Wn).$$

Increase of average wage:

$$I = \overline{w} \div \overline{W} = R_2 \times P_1 = R_1 \times P_2,$$

where

$$P_1 = \frac{S\,(Wn)}{S\,(n)} \div \frac{S\,(WN)}{S\,(N)} = \frac{S\,(Wn)}{m\overline{W}\overline{n}} \text{ and } P_2 = \frac{S\,(wn)}{S\,(n)} \div \frac{S\,(wN)}{S\,(N)}.$$

Then $P_1$ or $P_2$ measures the change in the average due to the shifting of numbers, while $R_1$ or $R_2$ measures that due to changes of wages.

Write

$$w_t = R_1.W_t + x_t, \quad n_t = \frac{\overline{n}}{\overline{N}}.N_t + y_t, \quad W_t = \overline{W} + \zeta_t,$$

so that $x, y$ and $\zeta$ measure the variation of $w, n$ or $W$ from their averages or weighted averages.

Then $\quad S\,(x_t N_t) = 0, \quad S\,(y_t) = 0, \quad S\,(\zeta_t N_t) = 0.$

It follows that

$$R_2 - R_1 = \frac{S(wn) - R_1.S(Wn)}{S(Wn)} = \frac{S\{(R_1 W_t + x_t)\,n_t\} - R_1.S(W_t n_t)}{S(Wn)}$$

$$= \frac{S\,(x_t n_t)}{S(Wn)} = \frac{S\left\{x_t\left(\frac{\overline{n}}{\overline{N}}N_t + y_t\right)\right\}}{S(Wn)}$$

$$= \frac{S\,(x_t y_t)}{S(Wn)}, \text{ since } S\,(x_t N_t) = 0, \ = \frac{1}{P_1} \times \text{Mean}\left(\frac{x_t}{\overline{W}}.\frac{y_t}{\overline{n}}\right).$$

Therefore $R_2 > R_1$ if increase in numbers is correlated with increase of wages in excess of $R_1$.

If $R_2 = R_1$ there is no net gain or loss by transference to *rising* or *falling* wages.

Also

$$P_1 = \frac{S\,(W_t n_t)}{\overline{W}.S\,(n_t)} = \frac{S\,\{(\overline{W} + z_t)\,n_t\}}{\overline{W}S\,(n_t)} = 1 + \frac{S\left\{z_t\left(\frac{\bar{n}}{\bar{N}}N_t + y_t\right)\right\}}{\overline{W}S\,(n_t)}$$

$$= 1 + \frac{S\,(z_t y_t)}{\overline{W}S\,(n_t)}, \quad \text{since} \quad S\,(z_t N_t) = 0,$$

$$= 1 + \text{Mean}\left(\frac{z_t}{\overline{W}}.\frac{y_t}{\bar{n}}\right).$$

Hence $P_1 > 1$, if $z_t$ and $y_t$ are positively correlated, that is if an increase in relative numbers is associated with *high* wages at the first date.

Similarly $P_2 = 1 + \dfrac{1}{R_1}\,\text{Mean}\left|\dfrac{v_t}{\overline{W}}.\dfrac{y_t}{\bar{n}}\right|$, where $w_t = \bar{w} + v_t$,

so that $S\,(v_t n_t) = 0$. $P_2 > 1$ if an increase in relative numbers is associated with high wages at the second rate.

With the help of these formulae we can obtain rough indications of the influence of the shifting of numbers on the general average over several periods.

Mr G. H. Wood[1] gives the following figures:

*Average money wages*

|  | Allowing for change in numbers | Not allowing for change in numbers |
|---|---|---|
| 1850 | 100 | 100 |
| 1880 | 147 | 131 |
| 1910 | 186 | 151 |

Taking the second column as $I$ and the third as $R_1$, we have

|  | $I$ | $R_1$ | $P_2$ |
|---|---|---|---|
| 1850–1880 | 1·47 | 1·31 | 1·12 |
| 1880–1910 | 1·265 | 1·15 | 1·10 |
| 1850–1910 | 1·86 | 1·51 | 1·23 |

Using the index $100:130$ for $I$ 1880–1910, as on p. 6 above, we have $P_2 = 1\cdot13$ for that period. Thus approximately half of the increase in average earnings is due to movement to higher wages, half to movement towards rising wages.

[1] *Journal of the Royal Statistical Society*, 1909, pp. 102–3, brought to a later date with the help of *ibid.* 1912–13, p. 220.

For the critical period that includes the War (1914 to 1924) we have more detailed calculations (*Economic Journal, loc. cit.*):

|  | 1914–1924 | | |
|  | Males | Females | All |
|---|---|---|---|
| $I$ | 1·95 | 2·10 | 1·98 |
| $R_1$ | 1·904 | 2·12 | 1·94 |
| $R_2$ | 1·906 | 2·12 | 1·94 |
| $P_1$ | 1·02 | 0·99 | 1·02 |

Here there was very little *net* change owing to the shifting of numbers. In fact the number of coal-miners increased, but these wages rose less than the average, thus neutralising the positive correlation in other industries. Women shifted from domestic employment to other work, not necessarily better paid.

For more recent periods we have the Reports of the Ministry of Labour in 1924, 1928 and 1931. Unfortunately these exclude agriculture and coal-mining in 1928 where the more important changes took place at earlier dates. Coal-mining is included in the 1931–5 column:

|  | 1924–8 | 1928–31 | 1931–5 |
|---|---|---|---|
| $I$ | 1·026 | 0·950 | 1·026 |
| $R_1$ | 1·023 | 0·943 | 1·018 |
| $R_2$ | 1·030 | 0·951 | 1·018 |
| $P_1$ | 0·996 | 0·999 | 1·008 |

$R_2$ is a trifle greater than $R_1$ in the first two periods, indicating some attraction to *rising* wages. In the last period there is a slight indication of attraction to *higher* wages.

Since all these index-numbers are computed on the basis of the averages within industries, they do not show the effects of the shifting of the relative numbers in different occupations within an industry, which may be important.

# Appendix C

## NOTES ON THE TABLE OF AVERAGE EARNINGS, p. 51

The statistics for 1924, 1931 and 1935 are computed from the Reports on the investigations of those dates, published in the *Ministry of Labour Gazette*, together with estimates for coal and agriculture.

The classification of industries follows that of the monthly returns of unemployment. Fishing is omitted. The last entry, 'other industries', includes non-metalliferous mining products, leather, 'other manufacturing industries', transport other than railways (except that 'other road transport' is omitted altogether), Local Government Service, and 'other industries and services'. Laundry and dyeing are included in clothing.

Distributive trades, commerce, etc., National Government, professions, and entertainments are predominantly to be classed as salaried occupations and are not included. Hotel, etc. service is omitted for want of data. The numbers insured under Local Government Service are used as weights for non-trading services, though salaried clerks are included here, because a considerable proportion are engaged in road cleaning and repairs; this over-weighting may be considered as balanced by the omission of 'other road transport'. It is to be remembered that these insurance figures are only used as weights, and considerable modification can be made in them without affecting the averages perceptibly.

The 1906 returns have been grouped as far as possible in the same way as the later ones, but the contents of the miscellaneous or residual group are somewhat different.

The returns as published for the 1924 and subsequent Censuses are for the average earnings of persons paid wages in selected weeks. Information is given about short-time, which is used as follows to estimate earnings in the full normal week:

**1924.** Cotton. Average earnings of males, 47s. 7d.; proportion on short-time, 17·2 per cent.; average number of hours lost by those who worked less than full-time, 14; hence average lost over all, 14 × 0·172 = 2·4 hours; normal hours, 48; full-time earnings,

$$47s.\ 7d. \times 48 \div (48 - 2\cdot4) = 50\cdot1s.$$

It is assumed that short-time is equally prevalent among males and females.

It will be noticed that over-time is ignored in this computation, and in some industries normal earnings are slightly over-estimated. Also in dock labour it appears probable that broken time is not sufficiently allowed for in the returns.

On the other hand, over-time is common on railways both in the traffic grades and in the shops, and the reduction on this account has been rather drastic before the figures have been included. The annual returns of railway wages and earnings give the averages for the normal rate and actual earnings in each occupation, but not the relative numbers in the occupations, so that a rather hazardous estimate has been necessary. At the one date for which there is a partial control (*Ministry of Labour Gazette*, 1926, p. 93), the over-time in traffic grades is put at 5·5 per cent., while the detailed figures here used allow for 13 per cent.

For coal it has been assumed that the normal number of shifts at full working is 11 per fortnight. The number actually worked is obtained as follows.[1]

Coal raised in last quarter of 1931, 55,191,000 tons.
Output per man-shift 21·86 cwt.
Hence number of shifts worked:

$$55,191,000 \div 1\cdot093 \text{ (tons)} = 50,620,000 \text{ in 13 weeks}$$
$$= 3,886,000 \text{ per week.}$$

Number of workpeople employed 799,374.
Hence shifts per person per week:

$$3886 \div 799 = 4\cdot86.$$

Earnings per man-shift, including 4·6d. average value of allowances, 9s. 7d.

---

[1] Data from *Ministry of Labour Gazette*, 1932, p. 171.

Hence actual earnings per week:

$$9s. \ 7d. \times 4.86 = 46s. \ 7d.^{[1]}$$

Full-time earnings:

$$9s. \ 7d. \times 5.5 = 52s. \ 8d. \text{ at } 11 \text{ shifts per fortnight.}$$

The net result of these adjustments is to raise the average of actual earnings only about 3 per cent. to get full-time earnings, and the difference is very nearly the same in 1924 as in 1931.

The figures now usually quoted for agricultural workers are the minimum county rates for ordinary labourers. Higher rates are paid to men in charge of animals, sometimes as a weekly rate, sometimes as minimum wages plus over-time. In recent years in the Board of Agriculture's Report on Proceedings under the Agricultural Wages (Regulation) Act, there have been estimates of actual earnings in a small number of cases. These indicate that average earnings for all workers are about 13 per cent. above the county minima. In both statements cash valuations of payments in kind are included. It is not clear whether special harvest rates are taken into account. This relation between standard rates for the ordinary labourer and average earnings for all classes is very much the same as before the war; there was a careful estimate in 1907. On the basis of this information estimates have been made for the table of average earnings at the dates taken. In using them with the rest of the table, it is implicitly assumed that this much over-time is normal in agriculture. But the agricultural average on p. 51 applies to men, while the other averages include boys. In 1935 the average for boys was about 11s. at 14 years up to 28s. 3d. at 20 years, the average over all being about 20s. In England and Wales about 20 per cent. of the male workers were under 21 years in 1935. Assuming that the boys got only the minimum wage, the average wage-earnings of all male agricultural workers were about 32s. 6d. per week in 1935, that is, 9 per cent. below the average for men. For purposes of computing the National Wage Bill the same relation may be assumed in other years.

These figures relate to England and Wales only. The inclusion of Scotland could not affect the averages seriously, since the number of males employed in agriculture in Scotland in 1935 was only 88,000 as compared with 594,000 in England and Wales, and the difference in average wages between the countries cannot be great.

[1] For the whole year the figures are $9s. \ 7d. \times 4.71 = 45.2s.$ (p. 51).

# Appendix D

## NOTES ON RETAIL PRICES

From 1914 onwards we have the well-known Ministry of Labour index-numbers of retail food prices and of the so-called cost of living. The published data are average prices of several kinds of food, and estimated average percentage changes for rent, clothing, fuel and light, and some miscellaneous articles. The changes are weighted on the basis of a collection of budgets made in 1904, slightly modified in 1914. The index does not cover the whole of working-class expenditure, except perhaps for the lower paid urban labourer, for there is an unallotted margin, which has increased in recent years, after payments for necessaries are met. It is applicable only to urban workers. For agricultural labourers a reasonable approximation may be made since 1914 by applying the price changes to agricultural budgets. From 1914 to 1918 the difference between the rise of prices as affecting the urban and the rural budgets respectively has been shown to be quite small (ref. 30, pp. 344–5). A similar calculation for 1936 results in index-numbers 129 to 133 (the margin being due to alternative systems of weights) in the case of the agricultural labourer for food, as compared with 129 for the urban worker. The agricultural cost of living index for the same date is 146 or 149 according to which reckoning is taken for food, if we assume the proportion of income spent on rent and clothing is the same as in the towns; if we reduce these proportions in the ratio 3 to 2, the index is 142 or 144. The town index is 146. Thus during the last twenty-two years there has been no significant difference in this respect between country and town.

It is unlikely that the new collection of budgets, as arranged for 1937, will result in any important modification of the estimates up to 1936 in the field of expenditure they cover, though it may be possible to test them by working backward with revised weights. It is hoped, however, that the new budgets will include a greater proportion of modern expenditure.

As we look back from 1914 the material becomes more and more deficient. There are two series of prices of food in London. One of these is the unweighted average of the changes of the prices of nine articles of food, and extends from 1877 to 1900. The other also refers to London only and extends from 1892 to 1914. (Both are given in the *Sixteenth Abstract of Labour Statistics*.) It is believed that the data for both series were mainly from large stores, where the movement may have differed from that in shops in working-class districts. There is no certainty that the movements in the provinces were the same as in London, especially at the earlier dates; but at the one relatively recent period at which comparison is possible, namely from 1905 to 1912 (*Sixteenth Abstract*, pp. 156–7, or Cd. 6955), the increases in food prices were nearly the same in London (12 per cent.) and in the average of provincial towns (13 to 14 per cent.).

In forming the index of food prices from 1880 to 1914 the London series have been used, the more complete one back to 1892, and the earlier one, recalculated with weights, from 1880 to 1892.

It is interesting to see how far these differ from the index of wholesale food prices computed by Sauerbeck and published annually in the *Journal of the Royal Statistical Society*. The dates selected are 1880 and 1914, the beginning and end of the series, 1892, where the less perfect series of retail prices ends, 1896, the year of minimum prices, and 1905 and 1911, where we have a guide from provincial towns; but here 1911 is used instead of 1912, because wholesale prices rose temporarily in 1912, while retail prices appear to have been little affected.

### *Index-numbers of food prices*

|      | Wholesale | Retail |
|------|-----------|--------|
| 1880 | 100 | 100 |
| 1892 | 77 | 80 |
| 1896 | 66 | 71 |
| 1905 | 73 | 80 |
| 1911 | 80 | 85 |
| 1914 | 80 | 87 |

It is seen that retail prices are estimated to have fallen less than wholesale to 1896, and that since then the movements have been roughly parallel.

In fact, the wholesale prices are not weighted at all strictly in accordance with retail purchases, and milk and other important foods are excluded, while sugar and coffee are over-weighted.

The index-numbers adopted for food from 1880 to 1914 are shown in the table on p. 121 below.

Analysis of the relation between retail prices of food and wholesale prices of as nearly as possible the same kinds of food, with the same system of weighting for both series, has been possible from 1914 onwards. The results are shown and the method explained in *Lloyd's Bank Monthly Review* (ref. 33).

It is found that the equation $p = 0.77P + 0.23$, where $p$ and $P$ are index-numbers of retail and wholesale prices respectively, is closely satisfied month by month from 1924 to 1933, most closely when a lag of two months is assumed between the movement of wholesale and that of retail prices. Here $p$ and $P$ are percentages of their averages in the period July 1924–December 1929.

This agrees with the assumption that in this period the contribution to a retail price of, say, 100s. was 77s. varying with wholesale price, and 23s. fixed cost of preparation and distribution. The period was one of nearly stationary wages. The equation

$$p = 0.77P + 0.23w,$$

where $w$ is an index of wages, has been examined with 1913 as base year. The procedure is rougher, for now $p$ is the index of all food included in the cost of living index, and $P$ is the general food index in the Board of Trade's wholesale price index. The results (hitherto unpublished) are as follows:

*Comparison of recorded and computed retail price index*

|          | 1913 | 1922 | 1923 | 1924 | 1925 | 1926 | 1927 | 1928 |
|----------|------|------|------|------|------|------|------|------|
| Recorded | 100  | 176  | 169  | 170  | 171  | 164  | 160  | 157  |
| Computed | 100  | 170  | 162  | 172  | 173  | 164  | 161  | 161  |

|          | 1929 | 1930 | 1931 | 1932 | 1933 | 1934 | 1935 |
|----------|------|------|------|------|------|------|------|
| Recorded | 154  | 145  | 131  | 126  | 120  | 122  | 124½ |
| Computed | 156  | 141  | 128  | 128  | 121  | 121  | 122  |

It is seen that the two series agree fairly well, except in the period of rapid movement prior to 1924.

An experiment can be made for the pre-war period, but there we have not such suitable wholesale prices as the Board of Trade index, and there are difficulties in getting satisfactory weights. An equation has been obtained, by the method of partial correlation, between the series of retail food prices on p. 121, Sauerbeck's index of wholesale food prices, and the wage series on p. 6.

We obtain            $p = 0.86P + 0.17w - 3,$

where $p$, retail price, $P$, wholesale price, and $w$, wages, are expressed in terms of their averages for the years 1880 to 1914.

The results are given in the following table, but for convenience the year 1900 is taken as 100:

### Retail prices

| | Recorded | Computed | | Recorded | Computed |
|---|---|---|---|---|---|
| 1880 | 129 | 128 | 1898 | 99 | 100 |
| 1881 | 125 | 125 | 1899 | 95 | 96 |
| 1882 | 124 | 123 | 1900 | 100 | 102 |
| 1883 | 125 | 123 | 1901 | 100 | 99 |
| 1884 | 116 | 109 | 1902 | 101 | 99 |
| 1885 | 105 | 104 | 1903 | 103 | 98 |
| 1886 | 102 | 101 | 1904 | 102 | 99 |
| 1887 | 99 | 100 | 1905 | 103 | 101 |
| 1888 | 100 | 102 | 1906 | 102 | 101 |
| 1889 | 102 | 106 | 1907 | 105 | 105 |
| 1890 | 101 | 104 | 1908 | 107 | 106 |
| 1891 | 103 | 110 | 1909 | 108 | 107 |
| 1892 | 104 | 104 | 1910 | 109 | 108 |
| 1893 | 99 | 103 | 1911 | 109 | 110 |
| 1894 | 95 | 96 | 1912 | 114 | 118 |
| 1895 | 92 | 93 | 1913 | 115 | 113 |
| 1896 | 92 | 91 | 1914 | 112 | 111 |
| 1897 | 95 | 95 | | | |

The agreement between the recorded series and that computed by the formula is quite satisfactory at the beginning and at the end, but there are aberrations in the central portions. The computed is high from 1887 to 1894, and low from 1901 to 1905. Evidently we have not the whole story, and the series do not refer closely to the relevant factors. This is not surprising, for the lists of food in the $p$ and $P$ series are not identical, and we have taken wages in general, not those appropriate to distribution.

The lower factor, 0.17, given to wages here, while 0.23 was given in the equation relating to 1913–35, suggests, but does not prove, that the wage element was relatively smaller before the War than after. The coefficients of correlation in the pre-war series were:

| | |
|---|---|
| Retail prices and wholesale | 0·94, |
| Retail prices and wages | − 0·20, |
| Wholesale prices and wages | − 0·38. |

If $w$ is ignored, the equation connecting $p$ and $P$ becomes

$$p = 0·80P + 20,$$

and the fit is not so good.

There has not been much investigation of this sort; but the reader may be referred to a study of the retail prices of bread and the wholesale prices of flour and wheat in the *Economic Journal*, 1913 (ref. 21). There results of a similar character are obtained, but the details and setting are different.

We could of course use one of these formulae for estimating the course of retail food prices before 1880, but it seems better to treat this only as one element in the cost of living, which we deal with in the next section.

## COST OF LIVING

Besides the change of food prices it is customary to consider the costs of rent, clothing and fuel as the other essential elements in the expenditure of the working class. A rather perfunctory entry is added for miscellaneous purchases; these are very difficult to define or price, and only a small weight is assigned to them in the British cost of living index.

From 1914 onwards we cannot do better than use the official index as our primary measurement; but in the period 1915 to 1923 its significance is so doubtful (ref. 51, pp. 72–5) that these years are not included in our estimates, and since we have not dealt with earnings in this period, there is no further loss by this exclusion.

From 1880 to 1914 the sources of information are the same as those for food.

*Rent.* In the "Second Fiscal Blue-Book" (Cd. 2337, 1904), there are estimates of working-class rents from 1880 to 1900. The more important figures relate to London and to a group of twenty provincial towns. In each case there are two sets of figures. One relates to the rents of a rather small number of identical houses throughout the period, the other to the average rent of all houses whose gross annual value was less than defined amounts, from which may be selected those less than £30 in London and £20 in the provinces. Both methods are open to objection. Identical houses may have deteriorated or improved in value, according to the condition of repair and to changes in the environment. An arbitrary upper limit, if it marked a class of houses at one date, would not apply to the same class at another when rents had risen. Analysis of the returns, however, shows that this crude measurement is fairly satisfactory. In particular we get virtually the same result in London, whether we take the limit at £30 or £50.

The best method seems to be to take the average of the four percentage changes, London and provinces, identical houses and rent below a limit. The four numbers are sufficiently close to make it indifferent what form of average is used; in fact, for 1880 as a percentage of 1900 we have for London, 88·8 for houses at less than £30, 88·5 for identical houses, and for the provinces, 85·2 and 92·7.

Of the increase, about one-third part is due to an increase in rates. For further calculations it is assumed that half of the increase in rates is of the same nature as rent, and the other half is for better service. This is discussed in the text, p. 29 above. For the general average for 1880, if the whole of rates is included we have 88·8, if none 92·9 or 93·6 according to the estimate of total rates adopted. From these data the percentage 91 is taken for 1880.

Similar computations have been made for 1885, 1890 and 1895, the only years for which we have data, and for intermediate years regular movements have been assumed.

The only other information is of rents in a great number of towns in the years 1905 and 1912 (repeated from Cd. 6955 in the *Eighteenth Labour Abstract*). Here it is seen that there was no significant change in rents in the eight years. In the absence of evidence of any change it seems best to assume stationariness from 1900 to 1914.

It is evident that the resulting series is liable to considerable error, even if we have a satisfactory definition; but since rent is taken as only one-sixth of expenditure, it needs an error of 6 in one of the serial numbers to make an error of 1 in the cost of living index.

*Clothing.* For clothing we have only estimates for the period 1881 to 1900 in Cd. 2337. These are on an insufficient basis, as is argued in the *Journal of the Royal Statistical Society,* 1905, p. 179. We must use them in default of better. To carry on this series the *Statist* wholesale price of textile materials has been used from 1900 to 1914. In this case an error of 8 per cent. is necessary to affect the cost of living 1 per cent.

*Fuel.* For fuel we have more reliable figures from the same sources as for food, and we have treated them in a similar way.

*Other expenditure.* Only a weight of 4 per cent. is allotted to miscellaneous goods in the existing cost of living index, and it is not of much importance what series we adopt, so long as its general movement is correct. We have used Sauerbeck's general index of the wholesale prices of materials as a rough measure of the changes.

The four series now explained have been weighted as in the existing cost of living index, the weights being applied to the year 1900, for purposes of calculation. In computing the average the weights given to food, rent, clothing, fuel and sundries are respectively 60, 16, 12, 8 and 4.[1] The table exhibits the series and the average. It is clear from the foregoing paragraphs that no great precision can be attached to the resulting series; it is only the result of making what appears to be the best practical use of admittedly imperfect data. The dates and the general nature of the changes are most probably adequately shown, and for short runs of, say, five years no modification of the hypotheses would make any significant differences. But in comparisons over longer periods it would be prudent to attach, say, ± 5 to one term of the ratio; thus from 1880 to 1914 we should read 114 : 109 ± 5, and we should say that in the thirty-four years the cost of living had fallen to an extent between 10 per cent. and no change, but that the statistics suggested a fall of 5 per cent. These limits just include the changes shown in the Board of Trade's account (Cd. 2337, p. 33) on the one side, and Mr Wood's estimate (p. 123 below) on the other, over the periods they cover.

When we wish to estimate the changes of the purchasing power of money before the year 1880, we can only proceed by working from

[1] Actually these apply when 100 is put for each series in 1904. In the series as printed the appropriate weights are 58·5, 15·9, 11·0, 10·1 and 4·5.

## TABLE XVII

### Series used in estimating an Index of Retail Prices

| Year | 1 Food | 2 Rent | 3 Clothing | 4 Fuel | 5 Sundries | 6 Weighted average 1900 = 100 | 7 Reduced so that 1914 = 100 | 8 Wholesale prices Food | 9 Materials | 10 Result of formula |
|---|---|---|---|---|---|---|---|---|---|---|
| 1880 | 129 | 91 | 108 | 74 | 105 | 114 | 105 | 125 | 95 | 105 |
| 1881 | 125 | 91 | 108 | 77 | 100 | 112 | 103 | 121 | 91 | 102 |
| 1882 | 124 | 92 | 107 | 73 | 100 | 111 | 102 | 119 | 91 | 102 |
| 1883 | 125 | 92 | 105 | 76 | 96 | 111 | 102 | 119 | 88 | 101 |
| 1884 | 116 | 93 | 103 | 75 | 91 | 106 | 97 | 105 | 83 | 95 |
| 1885 | 105 | 93 | 102 | 75 | 88 | 99 | 91 | 99 | 79 | 91 |
| 1886 | 102 | 93 | 102 | 73 | 84 | 97 | 89 | 96 | 76 | 89 |
| 1887 | 99 | 93 | 102 | 72 | 84 | 95 | 88 | 93 | 76 | 89 |
| 1888 | 100 | 93 | 101 | 73 | 86 | 96 | 88 | 96 | 78 | 90 |
| 1889 | 102 | 93 | 100 | 74 | 88 | 97 | 89 | 100 | 79 | 92 |
| 1890 | 101 | 93 | 102 | 80 | 89 | 97 | 89 | 97 | 81 | 91 |
| 1891 | 103 | 94 | 102 | 78 | 85 | 98 | 89 | 103 | 77 | 92 |
| 1892 | 104 | 95 | 101 | 78 | 81 | 98 | 90 | 97 | 73 | 89 |
| 1893 | 99 | 96 | 100 | 85 | 81 | 97 | 89 | 96 | 73 | 89 |
| 1894 | 95 | 96 | 99 | 73 | 75 | 92 | 85 | 88 | 68 | 84 |
| 1895 | 92 | 97 | 98 | 71 | 75 | 90 | 83 | 85 | 68 | 83 |
| 1896 | 92 | 98 | 99 | 72 | 75 | 91 | 83 | 83 | 68 | 83 |
| 1897 | 95 | 98 | 98 | 73 | 75 | 93 | 85 | 87 | 67 | 83 |
| 1898 | 99 | 99 | 97 | 73 | 74 | 95 | 88 | 91 | 69 | 85 |
| 1899 | 95 | 99 | 96 | 79 | 76 | 94 | 86 | 87 | 79 | 88 |
| 1900 | 100 | 100 | 100 | 100 | 100 | 100 | 91 | 92 | 91 | 94 |
| 1901 | 100 | 100 | 91 | 89 | 90 | 97 | 90 | 89 | 82 | 89 |
| 1902 | 101 | 100 | 92 | 85 | 89 | 98 | 90 | 89 | 81 | 89 |
| 1903 | 103 | 100 | 100 | 81 | 90 | 100 | 91 | 91 | 82 | 90 |
| 1904 | 102 | 100 | 108 | 79 | 90 | 99 | 92 | 91 | 82 | 90 |
| 1905 | 103 | 100 | 109 | 78 | 94 | 100 | 92 | 92 | 85 | 91 |
| 1906 | 102 | 100 | 121 | 79 | 104 | 102 | 93 | 92 | 94 | 94 |
| 1907 | 105 | 100 | 117 | 89 | 107 | 104 | 95 | 96 | 98 | 97 |
| 1908 | 107 | 100 | 94 | 86 | 90 | 102 | 93 | 96 | 84 | 92 |
| 1909 | 108 | 100 | 97 | 84 | 94 | 103 | 94 | 97 | 85 | 93 |
| 1910 | 109 | 100 | 111 | 84 | 101 | 105 | 96 | 99 | 92 | 96 |
| 1911 | 109 | 100 | 118 | 85 | 104 | 106 | 97 | 100 | 94 | 97 |
| 1912 | 114 | 100 | 118 | 87 | 110 | 109 | 100 | 108 | 100 | 101 |
| 1913 | 115 | 100 | 127 | 86 | 114 | 111 | 102 | 103 | 103 | 101 |
| 1914* | 112 | 100 | 126 | 86 | 110 | 109 | 100 | 100 | 100 | 99 |

\* First half-year.

The figures for the first six columns are as obtained in the text, and lead in column 7 to the Cost of Living index used in Chapter II. Columns 8 and 9 are Sauerbeck's wholesale index-numbers. Column 10 is obtained from these as explained in the text. The comparison is to be made between columns 7 and 10.

wholesale prices, for such retail prices as are known are too limited and sporadic for the purpose.

It is found that the series of index-numbers of the cost of living, as elaborated in the preceding paragraphs, has a close relation to the two series of wholesale prices of food and materials given by Sauerbeck. By the use of the method of partial correlation we find the equation $C = 33\cdot4 + 0\cdot32F + 0\cdot34M$, where $F$ and $M$ are Sauerbeck's index-numbers for food and materials, arranged so as to read 100 in the first half of 1914, and $C$ is the cost of living index computed from this formula. These values are shown in the table. When $C$ in the last column is compared with the weighted average shown in column 7, it is seen that there is close agreement, except perhaps in the years 1887–91 and the years of sudden inflation of wholesale prices, viz. 1900 and 1907. The formula is to be regarded as purely empirical, so that it is difficult to attach any significance to the three numerical expressions separately; indeed these values depend on the year in which the indices are equated to 100. (The last column was in fact computed from the data as originally given and worked to the first decimal place, and the series then raised proportionately to get the required date as basis; the numbers so obtained may differ by a unit from the nearest integer obtained by applying the formula directly to the numbers in the table.)

We can get an empirical estimate for earlier years by assuming that the same relation between wholesale and retail prices (and rent) applies before 1880 and after.

The resulting index-numbers are:

### Empirical estimate of the cost of living

1914 = 100

| | | | | | |
|---|---|---|---|---|---|
| 1846 | 106 | 1858 | 106 | 1870 | 110 |
| 1847 | 110 | 1859 | 108 | 1871 | 113 |
| 1848 | 96 | 1860 | 113 | 1872 | 120 |
| 1849 | 93 | 1861 | 112 | 1873 | 122 |
| 1850 | 94 | 1862 | 113 | 1874 | 115 |
| 1851 | 94 | 1863 | 115 | 1875 | 111 |
| 1852 | 96 | 1864 | 115 | 1876 | 110 |
| 1853 | 108 | 1865 | 113 | 1877 | 110 |
| 1854 | 115 | 1866 | 114 | 1878 | 104 |
| 1855 | 114 | 1867 | 114 | 1879 | 101 |
| 1856 | 114 | 1868 | 113 | 1880 | 105 |
| 1857 | 117 | 1869 | 111 | | |

Averages

| 1846–9 | 101 | 1865–9 | 114 |
| 1850–4 | 101 | 1870–4 | 116 |
| 1855–9 | 112 | 1875–9 | 107 |
| 1860–4 | 114 | | |

Mr G. H. Wood has given an estimate of the change in the cost of living from 1850 to 1902 in the *Journal of the Royal Statistical Society*, 1909, pp. 94–103, partly based on a former article (1902, pp. 665–90), and continued to 1910 by estimates based on later material (see 1912–13, p. 220). The data are fragmentary and most of them are not stated, so that it is impossible to criticise them in detail. He separated rent from commodities; for rent he assumed a uniform increase from 1880 to 1902, in all a rise equal to the greater of those discussed on p. 119 above. Commodities seem to be based principally on food, and the index is arrived at by taking the 'unweighted mean of a series of index-numbers for all commodities of ordinary consumption for which records are obtainable' (p. 95).

Over the period 1880–1910 his results may be compared with those adopted in the text as follows:

G. H. Wood:

| | Commodities | Rent | Cost of living |
|---|---|---|---|
| 1880 | 100 | 100 | 100 |
| 1910 | 91 | 115 | 96 |

Used on p. 121:

| | Food | Clothing | Fuel | Sundries | Commodities | Rent | All |
|---|---|---|---|---|---|---|---|
| 1880 | 100 | 100 | 100 | 100 | 100 | 100 | 100 |
| 1910 | 85 | 102 | 113 | 96 | 89 | 110 | 92 |

In the first lines commodities and rent are combined for the cost of living, with weights approximately 3 to 1. In the second the first four columns are combined to make commodities, by weights, respectively 15, 3, 2, 1, and commodities are combined with rent with weights in the ratio 21 to 4. The difference is thus mainly in the treatment of rent.

Though these figures have some use as showing the result of an alternative hypothesis, I do not think that they have so great a claim to validity as the more complete analysis given above (pp. 119–20), with the margins of error there discussed. The main difference in the results is prior to 1892. From 1892 to 1910 the increase in the cost of living index is 6½ per cent. by each method.

For earlier dates, if we equate Mr Wood's number to 105 in 1880, we have:

*Average*

|  | G. H. Wood | P. 122 |
|---|---|---|
| 1850–4 | 100 | 101 |
| 1855–9 | 110 | 112 |
| 1860–4 | 105 | 114 |
| 1865–9 | 110 | 114 |
| 1870–4 | 111 | 116 |
| 1875–9 | 107 | 107 |
| 1880 | 105 | 105 |

*Note.* Where we have budgets at two different dates for a class whose scale of preferences is assumed to be unchanged, we may measure the change of prices with equal plausibility on the basis of the earlier or of the later budgets.

Write $P_1 \ldots P_t \ldots P_n$ for the prices and $Q_1 \ldots Q_t \ldots Q_n$ for the quantities of the first budget, and $p_1 \ldots p_t \ldots p_n$, $q_1 \ldots q_t \ldots q_n$ for those of the second budget.

Then $I_1 = \dfrac{\sum\limits_{1}^{n} Q_t p_t}{\sum\limits_{1}^{n} Q_t P_t}$ and $I_2 = \dfrac{\sum\limits_{1}^{n} q_t p_t}{\sum\limits_{1}^{n} q_t P_t}$ are the index-numbers (usually multiplied by 100) on the two bases.

Since the claims of these two expressions are similar, it is reasonable to take some average of them. Professor Irving Fisher prefers the geometric mean (making of index-numbers). Good reasons can be given for using the expression $I_m = \dfrac{\sum (Q + q) p}{\sum (Q + q) P}$ (*Economic Journal*, 1928, p. 226; *Econometrica*, 1936, p. 31). When $I_1$ and $I_2$ are not far apart there is little difference between these averages, or from $\frac{1}{2}(I_1 + I_2)$.

It is reasonable to assume that when prices rise unequally expenditure is transferred from goods that appreciate specially rapidly to other goods, with or without a loss of satisfaction, and when prices are falling to those goods whose prices fall fastest.

Thus if goods $A$ and $B$ are to some extent substitutes for each other, we might have the following scheme:

*Rising prices*

|   | $Q$ | $P$ | $q$ | $p$ | $QP$ | $Qp$ | $qP$ | $qp$ |
|---|---|---|---|---|---|---|---|---|
| A | 2 | 100 | 1 | 140 | 200 | 280 | 100 | 140 |
| B | 4 | 100 | 5 | 110 | 400 | 440 | 500 | 550 |
| C | 4 | 100 | 4 | 120 | 400 | 480 | 400 | 480 |
|   |   |   |   |   | 1000 | 1200 | 1000 | 1170 |

$$I_1 = 1\cdot20,\ I_2 = 1\cdot17,\ I_m = 1\cdot185,\ \sqrt{I_1 I_2} = 1\cdot189.$$

*Falling prices*

|   | $Q$ | $P$ | $q$ | $p$ | $QP$ | $Qp$ | $qP$ | $qp$ |
|---|---|---|---|---|---|---|---|---|
| A | 2 | 100 | 4 | 60 | 200 | 120 | 400 | 240 |
| B | 4 | 100 | 2 | 90 | 400 | 360 | 200 | 180 |
| C | 4 | 100 | 4 | 80 | 400 | 320 | 400 | 320 |
|   |   |   |   |   | 1000 | 800 | 1000 | 740 |

$$I_1 = 0\cdot80,\ I_2 = 0\cdot74,\ I_m = 0\cdot77,\ \sqrt{I_1 I_2} = 0\cdot7693.$$

Write $$J_1 = \frac{\Sigma Pq}{\Sigma PQ}, \quad J_2 = \frac{\Sigma pq}{\Sigma pQ}.$$

Either of these is a measurement of the change in quantity bought from one date to another and is an approximation to the change in the standard of living.[1] By analogy with $I_m$, we may select

$$J_m = \tfrac{1}{2}(J_1 + J_2)$$

as a measurement (cf. ref. 30, p. 350, and ref. 25, p. 229).

Write $\dfrac{p_t}{P_t} = I_1 + u_t$, $\dfrac{q_t}{Q_t} = J_1 + w_t$, so that $u_t, w_t$ afford measurements of the differences from general averages of the price ratio and of the quantity ratio for one commodity.

Then
$$I_1 - I_2 = I_1 - \frac{\Sigma P_t Q_t (I_1 + u_t)(J_1 + w_t)}{\Sigma Pq}$$

$$= I_1 - I_1 \times J_1 \div J_1 - \frac{J_1 \Sigma P_t Q_t u_t}{\Sigma Pq} - \frac{I_1 \Sigma P_t Q_t w_t}{\Sigma Pq} - \frac{\Sigma P_t Q_t u_t w_t}{\Sigma Pq}.$$

[1] Note that $I_1 J_2 = I_2 J_1 = \dfrac{\Sigma qp}{\Sigma QP} = \sqrt{I_1 I_2} \cdot \sqrt{J_1 J_2} = $ approx. $I_m \cdot J_m$, where $J_m = \tfrac{1}{2}(J_1 + J_2)$. $\sqrt{J_1 J_2}$ is Prof. Irving Fisher's expression for change in quantity. In the numerical examples $J_1 = 1$.

It is readily seen that $\Sigma P_t Q_t u_t = \Sigma p_t Q_t - I_1 \Sigma P_t Q_t = 0$, and that $\Sigma P_t Q_t w_t = 0$.

$$\therefore I_1 - I_2 = -\frac{\Sigma P_t Q_t u_t w_t}{\Sigma Pq} = \Sigma P_t Q_t \left(\frac{p_t}{P_t} - I_1\right)\left(J_1 - \frac{q_t}{Q_t}\right) \div \Sigma Pq.$$

If then $u_t$, $w_t$ are positively correlated, $I_1 > I_2$.

Other forms can be given to these expressions. (See International Labour Office, *Studies and Reports*, Series N (Statistics), No. 20, *International Comparisons of Cost of Living*, 1934.)

It can be shown that where real income increases faster than wages we have $I_1 > I_2$ on the usual hypothesis that marginal utility decreases with increased possession.

The relevant formula is

$$I_1 - I_2 = \{\rho (i - \rho) + (1 + \rho) \Sigma r_t^2 w_t (-\eta_{tt})\} \div J_1.$$

Here $I_1, I_2, J_1$ have the meanings already given. $\rho, = I_1 - 1$, is the relative increase in prices. $i$ is the relative increase in expenditure. $r_t$ is the relative increase in the price of the $t$th commodity, $w_t$ the proportion of expenditure allotted to it.

$-\eta_{tt} = -\dfrac{p_t}{x_t} \cdot \dfrac{dx_t}{dp_t}$, the price elasticity of demand, where $x_t$, $p_t$ are the initial quantity and price.

By the hypothesis $\eta_{tt}$ is negative.[1]

Hence, if $\rho$ is positive, and $i > \rho$, that is, if income increases faster than prices, $I_1$ is greater than $I_2$, by a margin dependent on the 'substitutionability' between the commodities.

If income has risen less than prices, $I_1$ may be less than $\rho$, unless the deficiency is small and $\eta_{tt}$ considerable.

If prices are falling and $\rho$ is negative, the same conclusions apply when income has fallen less than $\rho$, for then $\rho$ is negative and so is $i - \rho$.

Thus, if we neglect the last term, and take, for example,

$$J_1 = 1\cdot10, \quad i = 0\cdot51, \quad \rho = 0\cdot40, \quad I_1 = 1\cdot40,$$

we have $\quad I_2 = 1\cdot40 - 0\cdot40 \times 0\cdot11 \div 1\cdot10 = 1\cdot36.$

---

[1] Cf. Allen and Bowley, *Family Expenditure*, pp. 141 *seq.* It is out of place here to discuss the limits of the applicability of this hypothesis.

# Appendix E

## NOTES ON THE INCREASE IN MIDDLE-CLASS OCCUPATIONS

It is fortunately not necessary for our purpose to attempt an exact definition of the middle class. Any reasonable classification can be made, so long as in an account of wages everyone on one side of the line is included, and in the complementary account of other incomes all on the other side are reckoned.

The broad distinction is between manual and clerical work, or what is nearly the same thing in manufacture, between administrative and operative employees, as made in the Censuses of Production. The middle class then contains all office work, and all professions, of which teaching is numerically the most important.

There are three major difficulties in classification. The Population Census does not clearly distinguish farmers, whose work is mainly directive, from those who do manual labour with their families on small holdings, and the position of working members of their families is ambiguous. In this case, only those described in the Census as farmers are taken as middle class, without distinction by the size of holdings.

A smaller number, whose position the Censuses do not make clear, is among those attached to professions, of which the most important are nurses, midwives, church officers. Here an arbitrary decision must be made.

Thirdly, there is the rapidly increasing class of shop assistants, not always distinguished from others engaged in distribution. In fact shop assistants are commonly drawn from the same families as typists and teachers in elementary schools on the one hand, while on the other the same families contain waitresses. The most convenient course is to include waitresses with domestic workers as wage-earners, and shop assistants (with certain exceptions) as middle class. Since little is known till quite recent times about wages or salaries in shops, this procedure allows the best estimate of wage changes.

The results may be summarised as follows:

TABLE XVIII

*Growth of the Middle Class. England and Wales.* Males

Numbers occupied in certain groups (in thousands)

| Year | 1881 | 1891 | 1901 | 1911 | 1911 | 1921 | 1921 | 1931 |
|---|---|---|---|---|---|---|---|---|
| Professions and administration | 248 | 289 | 343 | 408 | 477 | 530 | 598 | 535 |
| Commerce, clerks and miscellaneous | 397 | 514 | 694 | 908 | 823 | 881½ | 1647 | 2198 |
| Dealers and assistants | 652 | 765 | 915 | 1105 | 1080 | 862 | | |
| Employers not included above | 169 | 190 | 217 | 239 | 239 | 255½ | 445 | 445 |
| Farmers | 203 | 202 | 203 | 209 | 216 | 255 | 267 | 242 |
| Total | 1669 | 1960 | 2372 | 2869 | 2835 | 2784 | 2957 | 3420 |
| Others occupied | 6090 | 6846 | 7785 | 8587 | 8645 | 9298 | 9112 | 9827 |
| All occupied | 7759 | 8806 | 10157 | 11456 | 11480 | 12082 | 12069 | 13247 |
| Percentage middle-class of all | 21·5 | 22·3 | 23·3 | 25·0 | 24·7 | 23·1 | 24·5 | 25·9 |
| Middle-class growth | 100 | 117 | 142 | 172 | — | 169 | — | 195 |
| | — | 100 | 121 | — | — | — | — | — |
| | — | — | 100 | 121 | — | — | — | — |
| | — | — | — | — | 100 | 98·2 | — | — |
| | — | — | — | — | — | — | 100 | 116 |
| All occupied growth | 100 | 114 | 131 | 148 | — | 155 | — | 171 |
| | — | 100 | 115 | — | — | — | — | — |
| | — | — | 100 | 113 | — | — | — | — |
| | — | — | — | — | 100 | 105 | — | — |
| | — | — | — | — | — | — | 100 | 110 |
| Working-class growth | 100 | 112 | 128 | 141 | — | 152 | — | 163 |

If the middle class, taken as 1,669,000 in 1881, had grown at the same rate as the total occupied, it would have amounted to 1,669,000 × 1·71 in 1931. But it is estimated above that it had increased in the ratio 100 : 195. The excess increase was therefore 1,669,000 × ·23 = 400,000.

On the other hand, if we apply the 1931 percentage (25·9) of middle class of all to the 7,759,000 all occupied in 1881 we have 2,010,000, an excess of 340,000 over the then estimate.

A similar classification for females is as follows:

TABLE XVIII (*cont.*)

*England and Wales. Females*

Numbers occupied in certain groups (in thousands)

| Year | 1881 | 1891 | 1901 | 1911 | 1911 | 1921 | 1921 | 1931 |
|---|---|---|---|---|---|---|---|---|
| Professions and administration | 150 | 191 | 236 | 271 | 422 | 450½ | 437 | 414 |
| Commerce, clerks and miscellaneous | 52 | 89 | 151 | 263 | 144½ | 474 ⎫ | 1090 | 1300 |
| Dealers and assistants | 182 | 300 | 343 | 561 | 567 | 620½ ⎬ | | |
| Employers not included above | 23 | 27 | 27 | 29 | 29 | 22 | 20 | 23 |
| Farmers | 20 | 22 | 22 | 20 | 20 | 19½ | 19 | 17 |
| Total | 427 | 629 | 779 | 1144 | 1182 | 1586 | 1566 | 1754 |
| Others occupied | 2976 | 3317 | 3393 | 3687 | 3649 | 346 | 3471 | 3852 |
| All occupied | 3403 | 3946 | 4172 | 4831 | 4831 | 5054 | 5037 | 5606 |
| Percentage middle-class of all | 12·6 | 16·0 | 18·7 | 23·7 | 24·5 | 31·4 | 31·1 | 31·3 |
| Middle-class growth | 100 | 147 | 182 | 268 | — | 359 | — | 402 |
| | — | 100 | 124 | — | — | — | — | — |
| | — | — | 100 | 147 | — | — | — | — |
| | — | — | — | — | 100 | 134 | — | — |
| | — | — | — | — | — | — | 100 | 112 |
| All occupied growth | 100 | 116 | 123 | 142 | — | 148½ | — | 165½ |
| | — | 100 | 106 | — | — | — | — | — |
| | — | — | 100 | 116 | — | — | — | — |
| | — | — | — | — | 100 | 104½ | — | — |
| | — | — | — | — | — | — | 100 | 111½ |
| Working-class growth | 100 | 111 | 114 | 124 | — | 118 | — | 131 |

If the middle class had grown only at the rate of all occupied from 1881, it would have been 427,000 × (4·02 − 1·655) = 1,010,000 less than its estimate in 1931.

If in 1881 31·3 per cent. of all occupied had been middle class, as they were in 1931, it would have amounted to 1,065,000 instead of 427,000, an excess of 638,000.

*Note.* The figure for all occupied in 1891 is disturbed by the inclusion of farmers' wives as occupied at that date. Omitting them, we have for all occupied at the Census dates: 100, 110, 122, 140, —, 147, —, 163. The difference is unimportant, especially in view of the approximate nature of the results.

Under these guiding principles we use the available Census classifications. The classification has changed again and again, and it is impossible to find one that is uniform over a long period. It is necessary to take four separate periods: 1861 to 1881, 1881 to 1911, 1911 to 1921, and 1921 to 1931.

The first only allows summary treatment, but the result clearly shows that there was no essential change in the proportion of the middle to the working class in these twenty years.

For the second we have a table for England and Wales in Vol. x, Part 1, pp. 540 *seq.* of the 1911 Census, in which a classification is made uniformly for 1881, 1891, 1901, and 1911.

The classifications were altered radically in 1921 and no sufficient comparison with 1911 was made officially. It is, however, possible by merging broad groups to obtain a fairly reliable comparison of totals.

The 1931 Census was classified on nearly the same methods as that of 1921, and the results given in great detail; consequently for this period we can make precise comparisons on a clear definition.

For the whole period, 1861 to 1931, we have to piece together the four separate results. The only assumption practicable is that the percentage change that is measurable in any period is independent of the variation in definition, and we must therefore combine the changes by multiplication, and apply the result to the total computed in any one year.

## SPECIFICATION FROM THE 1911 CENSUS, USED FOR COMPARISON WITH 1881, 1891 AND 1901

### ADMINISTRATION AND GOVERNMENT

I. 1.2. Post Office Officers and Clerks, not telegraph or telephone.
    5. Other Civil Service Officers and Clerks.

II. 1.1, 2. Army Officers, effective or retired.
    2.1, 2, 4, 5. Navy and Marines Officers, effective or retired.

I. 2.2, 3. Municipal, etc. Officers; Poor Law Service.

PROFESSIONAL

III. 1.1, 2, 3, 4, 5. Ministers of Religion.
2.1, 2, 3. Lawyers and Law Clerks.
3.1, 2, 3. Doctors and Veterinary Surgeons.
4.1. Teachers.
5.1, 2, 3. Literature and Science.
6.1, 2, 3. Engineers and Surveyors and Assistants.
7.1, 2, 3, 4, 5, 6, 7. Artists, Musicians, Actors.

COMMERCIAL

V. 1.1, 2, 3, 4, 5, 6, 7. Merchants, Brokers, Salesmen, Travellers, Accountants, Auctioneers, Officers of Societies.
2.1. Commercial or Business Clerks.
3.1, 2. Bankers, Financiers.
4.1, 2. Insurance.
VI. 1.1. Railway Officials and Clerks.
2.1, 2. Cab and Garage Proprietors.
5.4. Telegraph and Telephone (including I. 1.1).

MISCELLANEOUS MIXED CLASSES

III. 1.6. Church Officers, etc.
3.5, 6. Nurses and subordinate Medical Service.
4.2. Others connected with Education.
7.7. Art, Music and Theatre Service.
8.1. Showmen, Games.
VII. 1.12. Agricultural Machines Proprietors and Attendants.
IX. 1.4, 5, 13, 14. Mines: Owners, Agents, Managers and Mine Service.
XXII. 4.5. Contractors, Manufacturers, etc., undefined.

AGRICULTURE

VII. 1.1. Farmers, Graziers.

DEALERS, INCLUDING SHOP ASSISTANTS

IX. 2.1, 2. Coal and Stone Dealers.

X. 11.1, 2. Ironmongers and other Dealers in Metals.

XIII. 1.8, 9. Furniture, Works of Art.
2.8. Timber.

XIV. 1.7, 8. Brick, China, etc.

XV. 3.4. Chemists.
4.8, 9. Oil and Colourmen, etc.

XVI. 4.1. Leather, Skins, etc.

XVII. 1.8, 9. Stationers, Dealers in Paper.
2.8, 9, 10. Publishers, Booksellers and Agents.

XVIII. 7.1, 2. Drapers.

XIX. 1.7. Hats; 1.9. Outfitters; 1.15. Haberdashers; 1.19. Boots;
1.24. Others.

XX. 1.2, 3, 4, 5, 6, 8, 10, 12, 16, 17, 20. Food.
2.2. Tobacconists.
4.1, 2, 3. Restaurant Keepers, Lodging-House Keepers.
Inn-Keepers.
4.9. Wine and Spirit Merchants.

XXII. 2.1. Cattle Dealers.
4.1, 2. Multiple Shops. Unclassified and General Dealers.
4.3. Pawnbrokers.

While some of these classes include manual workers, other classes not named include dealers.

The specification adopted for the comparison between 1911 and 1921 is essentially the same as the above, but some unimportant classes have been omitted and others added. This was done in order to make use of the comparison with 1921 made for all occupations in *Memorandum of the London and Cambridge Economic Service*, No. 17, Table IV (Occupational Changes in Great Britain, 1911 and 1921).

In that table the code numbers used in the 1921 Census are shown against the orders and sub-orders in the list above. Some adjustment was necessary for the present purpose, of which it is unnecessary to give details.

The Memorandum in question was officially criticised, and the table here used was withdrawn in a revised *Memorandum*, No. 17A; but it is believed that though the detailed comparisons in the table are in some cases uncertain, yet the totals obtained by merging many classes are at least approximately correct. In any case there is no other source of information.

For the comparison between 1921 and 1931 the 1931 Occupational Tables were used. In these it is easier than in any previous comparison to separate employers from wage-earners in manufacture and elsewhere. As a result the number of employers in 1921 is greater than was estimated in the 1911–21 comparison (see note below). In other classes the two estimates for 1921 are in reasonably close agreement. There was no intentional or unavoidable change in the selection.

*Note on the estimate of employers.* From Vol. x, Part I, Table 3 of the 1911 Census the number of persons classed as employers was added for all occupations not already included as middle class. This gave 239,000 males and 29,000 females. The proportion that these bore to the occupied population, excluding those already counted as middle class, was assumed to be the same in every Census from 1881 to 1921 inclusive. Unless the number of employers has increased at a definitely different rate from that of the number of wage-earners, the effect of errors in this hypothesis on the computed growth of the middle class is trifling. The percentage of the middle class to the total is, however, affected in the right direction.

Since the 1931 Census is readily available, it is only necessary to list the code numbers. The numbers were taken from the Occupations Volume, Table G, pp. 672 *seq.*

The code-numbers of the occupations (1931 Census) included as middle class are as follows: Agriculture, 010, 011, 015, 016. Employers, managers and officials in mining, manufacture and transport, 040, 041, 050, 051, 060, 061, 070, 080, 090, 100, 110, 120, 130, 240, 250, 270, 280, 290, 300, 340, 370, 380, 390, 400, 410, 430, 440, 450, 460, 480, 500, 520, 530, 540, 550, 560, 570, 580, 590, 610, 611,

612, 613, 630, 631, 632, 633, 634, 635, 636, 650, 910. Commerce, shops and clerks, 654, 655, 656 (telephones, etc.), 670 to 719 inclusive, 730 to 739 inclusive, 880 to 889 inclusive. Inns and lodging-houses, 861, 862, 864. Administration and defence, 740, 741, 742, 743, 750, 760, 761, 762, 764. Professions, 770 to 836 inclusive, 863.

We can extend the statistics in part to the United Kingdom for the period 1881 to 1911 by means of an abridged table, *General Report of the Census of England and Wales*, 1911, pp. 268 *seq.* Here only the major groups can be identified:

*Occupations in the United Kingdom (in thousands). Males*

|  | England and Wales | | | | Scotland | | | | Ireland | | | |
|---|---|---|---|---|---|---|---|---|---|---|---|---|
|  | 1881 | 1891 | 1901 | 1911 | 1881 | 1891 | 1901 | 1911 | 1881 | 1891 | 1901 | 1911 |
| Government, excluding police | 64 | 89 | 125 | 191 | 8 | 12 | 14 | 21 | 10 | 13 | 18 | 20 |
| Professions | 231 | 265 | 312 | 370 | 31 | 35 | 41 | 46 | 30 | 30 | 30 | 33 |
| Commerce | 308 | 396 | 530 | 663 | 44 | 54 | 66 | 76 | 22 | 28 | 35 | 39 |
| Farmers | 203 | 202 | 203 | 209 | 48 | 48 | 46 | 44 | — | — | — | — |
| Total | 806 | 952 | 1170 | 1433 | 131 | 149 | 167 | 187 | 62 | 71 | 83 | 92 |

| United Kingdom | 1881 | 1891 | 1901 | 1911 |
|---|---|---|---|---|
| Total of above (nearest 1000) | 1001 | 1171 | 1422 | 1712 |
| All occupied except Irish farmers | 9806 | 10903 | 12409 | 13818 |
| Percentage of above groups to all occupied: | | | | |
| England and Wales | 10·4 | 10·8 | 11·5 | 12·5 |
| United Kingdom | 10·2 | 10·8 | 11·5 | 12·4 |

Irish farmers are excluded throughout, since their status cannot be determined.

The groups included account for about half the middle class as defined for England and Wales in the previous tables, the principal omissions being shops and employers generally. It is seen that for the groups that are included the extension to the United Kingdom hardly modifies the percentages.

In the next table again about half the middle class is included. The percentages of the middle class in the limited number of groups increase rather more rapidly for the United Kingdom as a whole than for England and Wales, because these occupations grew at a later date in Scotland than in England.

For females the corresponding tabulation is as follows:

*Occupations in the United Kingdom (in thousands). Females*

|  | England and Wales | | | | Scotland | | | | Ireland | | | |
|---|---|---|---|---|---|---|---|---|---|---|---|---|
|  | 1881 | 1891 | 1901 | 1911 | 1881 | 1891 | 1901 | 1911 | 1881 | 1891 | 1901 | 1911 |
| Government | 7 | 15 | 26 | 45 | 1 | 2 | 2 | 5 | 1 | 3 | 4 | 3 |
| Professions | 187 | 243 | 295 | 347 | 16 | 21 | 31 | 36 | 20 | 23 | 25 | 32 |
| Commerce | 8 | 21 | 60 | 127 | 2 | 5 | 16 | 30 | 1 | 2 | 5 | 9 |
| Farmers | 21 | 22 | 22 | 20 | 7 | 7 | 8 | 7 | — | — | — | — |
| Total | 223 | 301 | 403 | 537 | 26 | 35 | 57 | 78 | 22 | 28 | 34 | 44 |

| United Kingdom | 1881 | 1891 | 1901 | 1911 |
|---|---|---|---|---|
| Total of above (nearest 1000) | 272 | 363 | 492 | 660 |
| All occupied | 4461 | 4880 | 5239 | 5797 |
| Percentage of above groups to all occupied: | | | | |
| England and Wales | 6·6 | 7·8 | 9·7 | 11·1 |
| United Kingdom | 6·1 | 7·4 | 9·4 | 11·4 |

The only other comparative information that is at least readily found in the Scottish Census Publications is a comparison of major groups between 1921 and 1931 in the Census of Scotland, 1931, Vol. III, p. xi:

*Occupations in Scotland (in thousands)*

|  | Males | | Females | |
|---|---|---|---|---|
|  | 1921 | 1931 | 1921 | 1931 |
| Administration, excluding clerks | 24 | 19 | 0 | 0 |
| Professions, excluding clerks | 43 | 46 | 45 | 49 |
| Commerce, excluding clerks | 117 | 151 | 84 | 96 |
| Clerks | 76 | 69 | 74 | 77 |
| Total | 260 | 285 | 203 | 222 |
| All occupied | 1543 | 1542 | 636 | 659 |
| Percentage of all occupied | 16·9 | 18·5 | 31·9 | 33·7 |

Though farmers are excluded because they are not separated from labourers, the numbers are considerably greater than in 1911 as shown in the previous table. In fact, the earlier classification is so incomplete that no comparison with 1911 can be made.

The growth of the middle classes as shown here from 1921 to 1931 is 100 : 110 for both sexes. In the more complete account for England and Wales it was 100 : 116 for males and 100 : 112 for females in the same period. We shall therefore make no great error if we adopt the English rates of growth for Great Britain and indeed for the United Kingdom, since it would take a great variation in the smaller countries to affect the rates of growth perceptibly.

The statistics resulting from the compilation of these data are:

*Great Britain. Occupied persons (in thousands)*

| Year | Males | | | Females | | |
|------|--------|---------|------|--------|---------|------|
|      | Middle | Working | All  | Middle | Working | All  |
| 1881 | 1982 | 6870 | 8852 | 476 | 3304 | 3780 |
| 1891 | 2319 | 7691 | 10010 | 711 | 3669 | 4380 |
| 1901 | 2814 | 8734 | 11548 | 908 | 3734 | 4642 |
| 1911 | 3389 | 9565 | 12954 | 1324 | 3998 | 5322 |
| 1921 | 3329 | 10283 | 13612 | 1764 | 3862 | 5636 |
| 1931 | 3844 | 10945 | 14789 | 1987 | 4209 | 6196 |

See also p. 134 above, where Ireland is included.

# Appendix F

## NOTES ON EARLIER ESTIMATES OF NATIONAL INCOME

In the *Economic Journal*, 1904, p. 459 (ref. 18), a table is given of income assessed to tax and of wages for the years 1860–1901, from which we select relevant dates.

| | Economic Journal £ millions | | Table XIII, p. 92 above £ millions | |
|---|---|---|---|---|
| Year | Income | Wages | Income | Wages |
| 1880 | 560 | 440 | 529 | 439 |
| 1896–1900 | 737 | 647 | 723 | 662 |

The differences for income are due to a change in the treatment of 'evasion' in the light of Stamp's elucidations. For wages the estimate of the number of wage-earners has been modified.

Intermediate income was not dealt with in the 1904 paper.

In the *Statistical Journal*, 1895 (ref. 1), the main subject was the change of wages from 1860 to 1891, but the National Income was estimated to make certain comparisons. The following details are taken from p. 248 of the *Journal*:

| | Statistical Journal £ millions | | | | Table XIII, p. 92 above £ millions | | | |
|---|---|---|---|---|---|---|---|---|
| | Income | | Wages | Total | Income | | Wages | Total |
| Year | Above £150 | Below £150 | | | Above £160 | Below £160 | | |
| 1880 | 652 | 126 | 567 | 1345 | 529 | 120 | 439 | 1088 |
| 1883 | 696 | 122 | 609 | 1427 | | | | |
| 1881–5 | | | | | 551 | 139 | 468 | 1158 |
| 1886 | 715 | 125 | 605 | 1445 | | | | |
| 1886–90 | | | | | 588 | 170 | 513 | 1270 |
| 1891 | 782 | 130 | 699 | 1611 | | | | |
| 1891–5 | | | | | 621 | 202 | 580 | 1403 |

The income figures used in the earlier estimate were the gross income without any reductions, and with a rather excessive allowance for evasion. (See *Economic Journal*, 1904, p. 465.)

The intermediate income does not increase, because with no computation of the numbers in the middle class was it assumed that a diminishing proportion were below the income-tax exemption limit. In the light of the statistics of p. 128 it now seems probable that there was some increase, though not necessarily in the proportion used in the interpolated figures in the table, p. 92.

It will be noticed that in the 1904 article the estimate of wages for 1880 was reduced more radically than that for income. It was found that the average figure for annual wages, which had been taken without due regard to its limitations from evidence given by Giffen to the Labour Commission, neglected unemployment, and perhaps made inadequate allowance for sickness, etc.; also the number of earners to which this average applied was taken as all persons occupied in manual work according to the Population Census, whereas in subsequent estimates this number was discounted. In fact, the £48 named as the average annual wage by Giffen was only used as a working figure to obtain the ratio of wages to income and especially its change. I gave there the caution 'this should not be criticised as an estimate of wages, but only as a step towards comparing the increase of wages with the increase of income; it should be noticed that all the estimates of actual amounts of wages as distinguished from those of their relative changes depend on Dr Giffen's 1886 estimate' (ref. 1, p. 247).

The object of the paper was to obtain index-numbers of wage changes, and its essence was comparison of similar returns, not, as had hitherto been done, absolute amounts. The index-numbers have been modified to some extent in the light of subsequent investigation. The totals have been completely discarded.

In *The Change in the Distribution of the National Income*, 1880–1913 (ref. 46), the estimate made for 1911 was brought up to date, modified a little and partly reclassified for the purpose of certain comparisons with earlier dates. The estimates can be shown in relation to those of the table, p. 92 above, as follows:

|  | Former estimates (£ millions) | | New estimates (£ millions) | |
|---|---|---|---|---|
|  | 1880 | 1913 | 1880 | 1913 |
| Income above £160 | 530 | 1030 | 530 | 1023 |
| Intermediate: | | | | |
|   Excluding shops | 120 | 305 | 120 | 340 |
|   Shop assistants | 10 | 60 | 10 | 60 |
| Wages | 465 | 770 | 430 | 797 |
| Total | 1125 | 2165 | 1090 | 2220 |

In the last column £20 Mn wages of soldiers and sailors abroad is included, which was ignored in the earlier estimate.

The higher figure for intermediate incomes in 1913 in the last column appears to be due to a different extrapolation of numbers after 1911, which may come from the statistics of occupation in the 1921 Census, not available for the earlier estimate. In any case it is a rather hypothetical estimate.

The main difference in the estimates is found in the Wage-Bill of 1880. In the earlier estimate it was deduced from the 1913 wage estimate by the index-number of wages and the change in the number of occupied persons. The former has been recomputed and together with allowance for unemployment accounts for about one-third of the difference. The revision of the estimate of the number employed accounts for the remainder. Unfortunately all the revisions act in the same sense, so that the relation of wages to the total is affected. The change, however, is small. If we include shop assistants as wage-earners (which is the better course here, since the estimate of their earnings as apart from those of other wage-earners in 1880 is quite hypothetical), we have

*Wages as percentage of total income*[1]

| Former estimates | | New estimates | |
|---|---|---|---|
| 1880 | 1913 | 1880 | 1913 |
| 42 | 39 | 40 | 38½ |

[1] The additions named on p. 92, note ‖ for pensions, undistributed agricultural income, etc. are not included in total income.

The following paragraphs are quoted from *The Change in the Distribution of the National Income*, pp. 10–11 (ref. 46).

"In the detailed report of the British Association Committee of 1910 it is estimated that there were 4,053,000 persons in the United Kingdom with incomes not assessed to income-tax and not generally classed as wage-earners, and that their aggregate income was £335 Mn and average income £84. This includes over 900,000 shop assistants and others with an aggregate income of £60 Mn who might reasonably be classed with wage-earners both in status and income, but in the earlier estimates they were not so classed.

"We cannot now improve on the earlier estimates, which are as follows:

Intermediate Income

| Authority | Date | Limit of income | No. of persons 000's | Aggregate income | Average income |
|-----------|------|-----------------|----------------------|------------------|----------------|
| Baxter | 1867 | £100 | 1497 | £81·3 Mn | £54 |
| Levi | 1866–7 | 150 | — | 120 | — |
| Levi | 1882–3 | 150 | — | 140 | — |
| Giffen | 1883 | 150 | 1800 | 118 | 66 |
| Committee | 1910 | 160 | 4050 | 335 | 84 |
| Committee amended | 1913 | 160 | 4310 | 364 | 84½ |

"The amendment to 1913 is due to a revision of the numbers and the inclusion of more salaried persons in industry.

"There is nothing inherently improbable in these estimates, and the authority and experience of their authors may be held perhaps to compensate the absence of detailed evidence, for there are many checks of a kind not easily expressed in numbers, which a statistician can bring to bear on estimates which in less experienced hands would be mere guesses. But the authors do not claim any high degree of precision, and we should be prepared to allow for an error of perhaps 20 per cent. in the number of persons and in their income in 1880. It may be suggested that the best account we can give for 1880 (taking the limit as £160) is:

Number of persons     1,500,000 to 2,000,000
Average income          £70
Aggregate income      £100 Mn to £155 Mn

while in 1913 we have 4,690,000 persons below £225 (viz. 4,310,000 below £160, and 380,000 between £160 and £225), with an aggregate income of £445 Mn."

The entry in the last paragraph of this quotation of the numbers and amount of income between £160 and £225 is made because the number of incomes above £160 had increased, with the general rise of income, by nearly 100 per cent, while the whole number of occupied persons had increased only 39 per cent.; the point £225 cuts off the same proportion of numbers of incomes, as nearly as can be estimated, as did £160 in 1880. We do not deal with this further now, because the question is merged in the treatment of middle-class income in general.

# Bibliography

The following lists contain the titles of nearly all the books and articles which I have written, separately or with colleagues, on the subjects of wages, prices or income. Not all of them have been referred to directly in the text.[1] The second part gives the exact references to the works of other authors to whom reference is made; it does not in any way claim to be a complete bibliography.

The principal sources of information are in official publications, which are named in the text as they are used.

[1] The opportunity is taken for making two corrections:

In *National Progress* (ref. 43), p. 13, last line, average wages in 1901 are stated as 27s. 6d.; it should be 26s. 6d. and the date 1902. The increase over 1881 should be 24, not 29, per cent. The mistake arose from a miscopy in the arithmetic.

In *National Income*, 1924 (ref. 47), on p. 21, table col. *d*, the first entry should be 1820, not 18200, and the consequent corrections should be made. This has no serious effect on the sequel.

## I. ARTICLES AND BOOKS BY A. L. BOWLEY

### Journal of the Royal Statistical Society

1. 1895. Changes in Average Wages in the United Kingdom between 1880 and 1891.

2–15. *The Statistics of Wages in the United Kingdom during the last hundred years*

2. 1898. Part I. Agricultural Wages.
3. 1899. Part II. Agricultural Wages in Scotland.
4. 1899. Part III. Agricultural Wages in Ireland.
5. 1900. Part IV. Agricultural Wages. Earnings and General Averages.
6. 1900. Part V. Printers.
7. 1900. Part VI. Wages in the Building Trades—English Towns.
8. 1900. Part VII. Wages in the Building Trades—Scotland and Ireland.

9. 1900. Part VIII. Wages in the Building Trades—Concluded. London.
10. 1902. Part IX. Wages in the Worsted and Woollen Manufactures of the West Riding of Yorkshire.

*With* GEORGE H. WOOD

11. 1905. Part X. Engineering and Shipbuilding. A. Trade Union Standard Rates.
12. 1905. Part XI. Engineering and Shipbuilding. B. Statements of Wages from Non-Trade Union Sources in General Engineering.
13. 1905. Part XII. Engineering and Shipbuilding. C. Statements of Wages from Non-Trade Union Sources in Shipbuilding and Engineering at Shipbuilding Centres.
14. 1906. Part XIII. Engineering and Shipbuilding. D. Dockyards and Railway Centres.
15. 1906. Part XIV. Engineering and Shipbuilding. E. Averages, Index-Numbers and General Results.

See also 87, below.

*The Economic Journal*

16. 1895. Wages in the United States and Great Britain.
17. 1899. Wages in the United States and Europe.
18. 1904. Tests of National Progress.
19. 1912. Wages and Mobility of Labour.
20. 1913. The Census of Production and the National Dividend.
21. 1913. The Relation between the Changes in Wholesale and Retail Prices of Food.
22. 1920. Cost of Living and Wage Determination.
23. 1920. Conditions of Employment of Dock Labour.
24. 1922. The Definition of National Income.
25. 1928. Notes on Index-Numbers.

*Journal of the Royal Statistical Society*

26. 1910–11. Report of a Committee of the British Association. The Amount and Distribution of Income (other than wages) below the income-tax exemption limit in the United Kingdom.

27. 1912. Measurement of Employment.
28. 1913. Working-class Households in Reading.
29. 1914. Rural Population in England and Wales.
30. 1919. The Measurement of Changes in the Cost of Living.

### Other Journals

31. 1914. *Quarterly Journal of Economics.* The British Super-Tax.
32. 1929. *The Banker.* The Low Birth-Rate and Unemployment.
33. 1930. *Lloyds' Bank Monthly Review.* The Relation between Wholesale and Retail Prices.
34. 1933. *Econometrica.* The Action of Economic Forces in Producing Distributions of Income, Prices and other Phenomena.
35. 1921. *Economica.* Earners and Dependents in English Towns.
36. 1922. *Economica.* The Relation between Wholesale and Retail Prices since the War.
37. 1928. *Economica.* Some tests of the Trustworthiness of Public Statistics.

### London and Cambridge Economic Service. Memoranda

38. 1924. Mem. V. Relative Changes in Price and other Index-Numbers.
39. 1924. Mem. VII. Seasonal Variations in Finance, Prices and Industry.
40. 1926. Mem. XVII. Occupational Changes in Great Britain, 1911 and 1921.
41. 1926. Mem. XVIIA. Numbers Occupied in the Industries of England and Wales, 1911 and 1921.
42. 1931. Mem. XXVIII. A New Index-Number of Wages.

### Pamphlets

43. 1904. *National Progress in Wealth and Trade.* P. S. King.
44. 1914–15. *Prices and Earnings in Time of War.* Oxford Pamphlets.
    *The War and Employment.* Oxford Pamphlets.
45. 1919. *The Division of the Product of Industry.* Oxford University Press.
46. 1920. *The Change in the Distribution of the National Income, 1880–1913.* Oxford University Press.

47. 1928. With Sir J. STAMP: *The National Income, 1924.* Oxford University Press.

## Books

48. 1900. *Wages in the United Kingdom in the Nineteenth Century.*
49. 1909. *An Elementary Manual of Statistics.*
50. 1915. *The Measurement of Social Phenomena.*
51. 1921. *Prices and Wages in the United Kingdom, 1914–1920.*
52. 1930. *Some Economic Consequences of the Great War.*
53. 1915. With A. R. BURNETT-HURST: *Livelihood and Poverty.*
54. 1925. With M. HOGG: *Has Poverty Diminished?*

## As a member of a Committee

55. 1923. *The Third Winter of Unemployment.*
56. 1924. *Is Unemployment Inevitable?*
57. 1932. Vol. III, *New Survey of London Life and Labour.*
58. 1934. Vol. VI, *New Survey of London Life and Labour.*
59. 1935. Sequel to 57 and 58. *Economica.* The Occupations of Fathers and of their Children.
60. 1935. Sequel to 57 and 58. *Statistical Journal.* Number of Children in Working-class Families in London, 1929–30.
61. 1936. Sequel to 57 and 58. *Statistical Journal.* Effect of Modifying the Poverty Line.

## Encyclopaedias

62. 1899. Palgrave's *Dictionary of Political Economy.* Wages, Nominal and Real.
63. 1908. Appendix to above. Changes in Nominal and Real Wages in the United Kingdom since 1850.
64. *Encyclopaedia Britannica*, xth, xiith, xiiith and xivth Editions. Articles on Wages, Cost of Living, Prices and Index-Numbers.
65. Bibliography of books, etc. relating to wages and hours throughout the nineteenth century, in the *Economic Review* (The Journal of the Christian Social Union), Oct. 1898 (with Miss Hopkinson).

There is also a bibliography in ref. 48, Appendix III.

## II. AUTHORS

66. BEVERIDGE, SIR W. H. Mr Keynes' evidence for Over-population. *Economica*, 1924.
67. BOOTH, CHARLES. *Life and Labour of the People*. 1892 *seq.*
68. BROWN, F. Expenses of Production in Great Britain. *Economica*, 1928.
69. CLARK, COLIN. *The National Income*, 1924–1931. 1932.
70. CLARK, COLIN. *National Income and Outlay*. 1937.
71. CONNOR, L. R. On certain Aspects of the Distribution of Income in the United Kingdom in 1913 and 1924. *Statistical Journal*, 1928.
72. FLUX, Sir A. The National Income. *Statistical Journal*, 1929.
73. FORD, P. *Work and Wealth in a Modern Port*. 1934.
74. GEORGE, R. F. A New Calculation of the Poverty Line. *Statistical Journal*, 1937, pp. 74–95.
75. GIFFEN, R. *Essays in Finance*, Second Series, 1890. X. The Progress of the Working Classes in the last half-century. XI. Further Notes on the Progress of the Working Classes. (Also printed in the *Statistical Journal*, 1883, 1886.)
76. HILL, A. B. A Physiological and Economic Study of the Diets of Workers in Rural Areas as compared with those of Workers resident in Urban Districts. *Journal of Hygiene*, Oct. 1925.
77. JONES, D. CARADOG (edited by). The Social Survey of Merseyside, 1934.
78. MACKENZIE, W. A. Changes in the Standard of Living in the United Kingdom, 1860–1914. *Economica*, 1921.
79. ORR, Sir JOHN BOYD. *Food, Health and Income*. 1936.
80. RAMSBOTTOM, E. C. The Course of Wage Rates in the United Kingdom, 1921–1934. *Statistical Journal*, 1935.
81. ROWNTREE, B. S. *Poverty. A Study of Town Life*. 1902.
82. ROWNTREE, B. S. *The Human Needs of Labour*. 1918 and 1937.
83. STAMP, J. C. *British Incomes and Property*. 1916.
84. STAMP, Sir JOSIAH. The Influence of the Price Level on the Higher Incomes. *Statistical Journal*, 1936.

85. TAUSSIG, F. W. Great Britain's Foreign Trade Terms after 1900. *Economic Journal*, 1925.

86. WOOD, G. H. Real Wages and the Standard of Comfort since 1850. *Statistical Journal*, 1909.

87. WOOD, G. H. The Statistics of Wages in the United Kingdom during the nineteenth century. Parts XV to XIX. The Cotton Industry. *Statistical Journal*, 1910.

88. WOOD, G. H. Examination of some Statistics relating to the Wool Textile Industry. *Statistical Journal*, 1927.

89. WOOD, G. H. Stationary Wages-rates. *Economic Journal*, 1901.

90. A Survey of the Standard of Living in Sheffield. Sheffield Social Survey Committee. *Survey Pamphlet*, no. 9. Prepared by A. D. K. Owen.

91. *A Social Survey of Plymouth*, 1935.

# Index

Printed in the United States
By Bookmasters